STAND
on the
WORD
Study Guide

JOSHUA

A 15-Day Journey through the Word

with Tony Perkins

FIDELIS PUBLISHING ®

ISBN: 9781956454802

Joshua: Finish Strong!
A Stand on the Word Study Guide

Content contributor: Dr. Kenyn Cureton
Cover design: Diana Lawrence
Interior layout design/typesetting: Lisa Parnell
Copyeditor: Lisa Parnell

Order at www.faithfultext.com for a significant discount. Email info@fidelis publishing.com to inquire about bulk purchase discounts.

Fidelis Publishing, LLC Sterling, VA•Nashville, TN www.fidelispublishing.com

Maps' geographic features courtesy of Bible Mapper (www.biblemapper.com).

Manufactured in the United States of America

10 9 8 7 6 5 4 3 2 1

FIDELIS
PUBLISHING

Contents

— Day 1 —

Joshua: An Introduction

Welcome to the Stand on the Word Study Guide on Joshua! For me, the book of Joshua is for the Old Testament sort of like the book of Ephesians is for the New Testament because both offer practical insight on how we, as followers of Christ, are to fight the good fight of faith. Before we dive into our study of Joshua, let's consider the background and a brief overview. The book of Joshua continues the story of the Israelites after their exodus from Egypt and wilderness wanderings, with the focus on taking the promised land. In fact, the purpose of the book of Joshua is to tell us how to be successful in taking possession of God's promise. And that begins and ends with trusting and obeying God and His Word: "Only be strong and very courageous, that you may observe to do according to all the law which Moses My servant commanded you; do not turn from it to the right hand or to the left, that you may prosper wherever you go" (Josh. 1:7).

Most Old Testament scholars believe Joshua recorded (or directed a scribe to record) the vast majority of the book. In fact, early chapters include firsthand accounts with personal pronouns (e.g., 5:1, 6). Plus, the book is full of military strategy, tactics, and details that God's general, Joshua, obviously directed. Added to this is the fact 24:26 refers to Joshua writing down the law of God. It stands to reason if Joshua could copy at least Deuteronomy, if not the entire Torah, he could have written most of the book that bears his name as well. In fact, the Jewish Talmud claims Joshua wrote his own book and eight verses in the Torah, which describe the death of Moses.[1] However, the rabbis added that Phineas the priest likely contributed some of the materials about events after the conquest (15:13–19; 19:47; 24:29–33) and wrapped up the book.

The events of the book of Joshua span about twenty-five to thirty years, starting soon after the death of Moses (1:1) around 1406 BC. It begins with the Lord commissioning Joshua as the new leader with the nation of Israel poised on the banks of the Jordan River, across from Jericho. Once the conquest commenced, it took about seven years to break the main force's resistance. In the middle of this, the covenant with Yahweh was renewed for a new generation at Shechem, then the land was apportioned, and mop-up operations continued through the end of the book. Joshua's final address and subsequent death came almost thirty years after combat operations began. Four words summarize the division of the book of Joshua's twenty-four chapters: *cross*, *take*, *divide*, and *serve*:

- Chapters 1–5: "Cross the Jordan into the land I have given you."
- Chapters 6–12: "Take the land I have given you."
- Chapters 13–21: "Divide the land I have given you."
- Chapters 22–24: "Serve the Lord in the land I have given you."

The Hebrew name *Joshua* means, "Yahweh is salvation." In fact, Joshua is the same New Testament name for Jesus. Consequently,

Joshua is a type of Jesus. Moses was the lawgiver, and he was unable to bring the children of Israel into the promised land, which illustrates that the law cannot save us. We're saved by grace through faith in the greater Joshua, Jesus Christ. So what does the promised land represent? Does it represent heaven, as some songs suggest, or does it represent the abundant life that Jesus came to give us? I believe it is the latter. When the children of Israel went into the promised land, they had to do battle. They had to deal with sin, evil, and compromise as they crossed into the promised land. Heaven will know none of those things.

Consequently, I believe the promised land represents what we have here and now as believers in Jesus Christ, that abundant life. We enter into the abundant life totally by God's grace, through Jesus Christ. But to experience the fullness of the promise, we must occupy through faith, obedience, and action, which is what we see throughout the book of Joshua. One of the most admirable qualities of Joshua is that of all the Old Testament figures: he finished strong. We don't really see many mistakes that Joshua made along the way, but at the end of his life, we see him as a man who was finishing strong, which is encouraging. How did he do it? He did it by yielding to the Word and ways of God.

I have a few additional foundational observations before we begin the book. Joshua was from the tribe of Ephraim. Some scholars believe he had actually served in the Egyptian army, and it was not uncommon for a foreign slave to serve in the military. And we'll see in this book that Joshua was a tremendous military strategist. In fact, military leaders even to this day study Joshua's tactics. He was 40 years old when the exodus occurred and 80 years old when he was commissioned. Like Moses, he destroyed the retirement concept; there was no such thing. Joshua died at the age of 110. We will see leadership qualities Joshua displayed throughout this book that are worthy of emulation: faith, courage, obedience, and devotion to the Word of God. Joshua gives us a great road map for successful Christian living. At the end of the book, Joshua presents loyalty to the Lord as a choice—one we must make as well, a stand we must take. May we declare with Joshua, "as for me and my house, we will serve the LORD" (24:15c).

How to Get the Most from the Study Guide

While the study guide offers spiritual insights and applications, the real impact comes from the words of Scripture, which is the Word of God. Please read the selected text for the day in your own Bible. God's Word is living and active (Heb. 4:12). The Spirit of God uses His Word to change your life. Nothing else can do that. So before reading the daily commentary, read God's Word! In fact, here are five habits to cultivate as you approach God's Word each day.

1. ***Read it through:*** Don't skip around. Read the entire selection of Scripture. If you are pressed for time, please read the Bible before you read the study guide notes. So read it through.
2. ***Think it over:*** Meditate on it. Let it marinate in your mind. If you can, take notes. We provide a notes page at the end of each day. Think it over.
3. ***Pray it in:*** Personalize the Scripture. Turn the verse that speaks to you into a prayer, and then pray it into your life. Ask God what you need to do in response. This leads to the next habit.
4. ***Live it out:*** Consider ways to apply what God is revealing to you, ways you can obey Him. Put His Word into practice. Make it a part of who you are, how you think, how you

speak, and behave toward God and other people. In other words, take God's Word and live it out.

5. ***Pass it on.*** Don't keep it to yourself. There are people in your life who need the same truth God has spoken to you in His Word. Share it. Pass it on.

About Stand on the Word

Stand on the Word is a ministry of Family Research Council, whose mission is to serve in the kingdom of God by championing faith, family, and freedom in public policy and the culture from a biblical worldview. The purpose of Stand on the Word is to lay the foundation for a biblical worldview through daily reading and application of God's Word. For the daily journey, we have created a chronologically prioritized reading plan through the entire Bible that can be accessed at frc.org/Bible or simply by texting the word *Bible* to 67742.

— Day 2 —

Today's Reading: Joshua 1

Verse of the Day

> "Only be strong and very courageous, that you may observe to do according to all the law which Moses My servant commanded you; do not turn from it to the right hand or to the left, that you may prosper wherever you go."
>
> *Joshua 1:7*

Please read the entire Scripture selection in your own Bible and highlight or underline verses that stand out to you before you read the observations and engage the questions below.

Let's begin in Joshua 1:1–2a: "After the death of Moses the servant of the LORD, it came to pass that the LORD spoke to Joshua the son of Nun, Moses' assistant, saying: 'Moses My servant is dead.'" Think about what a seismic change this was for Israel. For forty years they knew every morning they would wake up with Moses at the helm, manna would be there for breakfast, and the pillar of cloud would lead them by day and the pillar of fire by night. They had the routine down out there in the wilderness, but things were going to change. No more Moses, no more pillar of cloud or fire to guide them, and soon no more manna. They were about to start all over again. Joshua was the new leader for a new day in a new land. But even Joshua must have been fearful about the future because God told him four times here in this chapter to be strong and courageous (vv. 6, 7, 9, 18).

Israel was poised on the very threshold of this awesome assignment to take the land, and God gave Joshua a command and a wonderful promise: "Now therefore, arise, go over this Jordan, you and all this people, to the land which I am giving to them—the children of Israel. Every place that the sole of your foot will tread upon I have given you, as I said to Moses" (vv. 2b–3). Notice it is past tense. It is already a done deal. You say, "Wait a minute. They weren't even in the land yet. They haven't even crossed Jordan." And yet God had already given the victory to them! God's promises in Scripture to us are not ours until we act upon it. We must stand on the promises with action to claim what God has given us. They could have said, "The Lord has given us the promised land," but if they had stayed on the other side of the Jordan, they never would have taken possession of the promised land. Faith without works is dead. Faith claims without action are simply bluster.

God followed that promise with an even greater one, the promise of His presence: "No man shall be able to stand before you all the days of your life; as I was with Moses, so I will be with you. I will not leave you nor forsake you" (v. 5). And just to make sure Joshua got it, He repeated it: "[D]o not be afraid, nor be dismayed, for the LORD your God is with you wherever you go" (v. 9b). Those are amazing promises, but what does God want us to do? He referenced the land and even marked off the boundaries and told them He had already given it to them. Then God gave Joshua a series of commands. Look at verses 7–8:

> "Only be strong and very courageous, that you may observe to do according to all the law which Moses My servant commanded you; do not turn from it to the right hand or to the left, that you may prosper wherever you go. This Book of the Law shall not depart from your mouth, but you shall meditate in it day and night, that you may observe to do according to all that is written in it. For then you will make your way prosperous, and then you will have good success."

Basically, God told Joshua concerning the law He handed down to Moses and that Moses handed down to Joshua, "This is your instruction manual that will be your guide. This will provide direction." The key to giving direction is all wrapped up in the Word of God. In order to provide your family with direction, you need to consult that manual. And there is a promise for those who do as God commands: "For then you will make your way prosperous, and then you will have good success."

But before we get to the promise, let's make sure we meet the conditions. God had three requirements for Joshua and for us if we want to enjoy the kind of success and victory He intends for us:

***1. The Word of God should be in our mouth*:** In other words, we are to verbalize the Word of God. We are to speak it, not just read it. Not just memorize it. We should verbalize it in order to vitalize it, to make it real. We should speak the Word of God. There is something quite powerful about taking God's words and speaking them. When Jesus was tempted in the wilderness, Satan tried to deceive and destroy Him three times. Jesus responded three times, verbalizing the Word of God (Matt. 4:1–11). He quoted Deuteronomy 8:3, then 6:16, and finally 6:13. Jesus took God's Word from the law Moses handed to Joshua and spoke it to Satan, and Satan was defeated! Learn to verbalize God's Word, not only to overcome temptation but to provide direction. Remember, the psalmist said, "Your word is a lamp to my feet and a light to my path" (119:105). So this is the first key to success—to have the Word of God in your mouth. But not only should it be in your mouth; it needs to be in your mind.

***2. The Word of God must be on our mind*:** Look at this portion of verse 8 again: "you shall meditate in it day and night." The message: Get the Word of God into our mind. Meditate on the Word of God. The original Hebrew word for "meditate" has in it the idea of humming. The Word of God is to be like a tune stuck in our head. Have you ever heard some song in the morning, and then you find yourself humming it all day long? That's the idea of meditating on the Word of God. Now I know what you are thinking: *Me, memorize chapters of the Bible?* I hear you, but don't tune out just yet. Try starting with one verse a week. Enter it as a note on your phone and review it. Put it on a sticky note on your mirror you use in the morning. Practice saying it every day. In fact, it says here in verse 8, "meditate in it day and night." Take that verse and think about it, ponder it, and ask God, "What are You saying to me? What does that mean? How does this apply to me? What does this mean for my family and the direction we should go?" Hopefully by the end of the week it will become a part of you. And then you can impart it to your family and friends to provide encouragement and direction. So the Word of God is to be in our mouths and on our minds. Here's the third key to success.

***3. The Word of God is to be in our manners*:** That is our behavior, the way we act, our conduct. Look back at verse 8: "that you may observe to do according to all that is written in it." That means to meditate on God's Word with the purpose of obeying it. See Bible study and meditation doesn't really give knowledge of God. Bible study gives knowledge about God, but obedience gives knowledge of God. Jesus said, "He who has My commandments and keeps them, it is he who loves Me. And he who loves Me will be loved by My Father, and I will love him and manifest Myself to him" (John 14:21). And when we obey, Jesus will become real! When we obey, the Bible will literally come alive with meaning, purpose, and direction. So, basically, God said to Joshua, "Take the book of the law, take My Word as your map, manual, and guidebook; and not only is it to be in your mouth and on your mind, it is to impact your manners, the way you live." In other words, it should change our character and our conduct. Consequently, we're not just to read the Bible simply for information but ultimately for transformation. It is to change our way of life! We are to read it, study it, and then do it!

As you open the Bible every day, I encourage you to pray, "Lord, show me today what You want me to see and do. Show me how to conform my life to Your will and Your ways. Lord, I commit myself today that whatever You say to me I will do it with Your help. Whatever direction You send me, there I will go. And God help me give my family Your direction." That's what you ought to pray as you open the Word of God daily. Expect God's direction not only for your life but also for your marriage, children, grandchildren, church service, career, citizenship, and so on. Citizenship? Yes, God's Word even provides direction on how to vote! Let God's Word guide you in every area of life.

To me, Joshua 1:7–8 contain the most important spiritual truth that we'll find in this book. And that's saying a lot because a lot is in the book of Joshua. Strength and courage were needed not to face opponents that occupied the land. Strength and courage were needed to obey God. If we obey Him, He has promised to take care of the rest and to rout the opposition. Now you might say, "Oh, that's easy, isn't it?" It is easy to obey God when we're living in easy times. But it isn't so easy to obey God when we're living in times when the people have rejected God and His Word and when they mock and ridicule those who seek to live by God's transcendent truth. God's ways have always been counter to the popular culture, but it has never been more pronounced in my life than what we see right now.

It takes courage not to say you're a Christian but to live a life according to God's Word as a Christian. Think about the courage and humility Joshua had to have to serve as a military leader in this first campaign in the conquest of the promised land, which we'll read about later. And that was Jericho—to march around it for seven days, blowing trumpets. What kind of military campaign was that? It is what God told Joshua to do, and that's what made him unique and successful. Now here is a truth that will make all the difference in living the abundant life: If you fear or revere God, you won't stand in fear of man. Remember, He is with you wherever you go.

Questions for Reflection and Discussion

1. What encouragement did God repeat four times to Joshua (see vv. 6, 7, 9, 18)?

2. What was God's formula for success (see v. 8)?
    a. Speak the Word of God
    b. Meditate on the Word of God
    c. Obey the Word of God
    d. All of the above

Notes on Today's Bible Reading

— Day 3 —

Today's Reading: Joshua 2

Verse of the Day

> "And as soon as we heard these things, our hearts melted; neither did there remain any more courage in anyone because of you, for the LORD your God, He is God in heaven above and on earth beneath."
>
> *Joshua 2:11*

Please read the entire Scripture selection in your own Bible and highlight or underline verses that stand out to you before you read the observations and engage the questions below.

Today we are in Joshua 2. The chapter begins with Joshua giving two of his men a mission: "Now Joshua the son of Nun sent out two men from Acacia Grove to spy secretly saying, 'Go, view the land, especially Jericho'" (v. 1a). This was nothing new for Joshua. You might recall he was a member of the original twelve-man recon unit that spied out the promised land forty years before, as recorded in the book of Numbers. God told Moses to choose a leader from each tribe to investigate the land and the opposition (Num. 13:18–20). Now that they were on the edge of the promised land forty years later, Joshua resorted to sending out another recon team for the same purpose. Yet notice Joshua did not send out a committee of twelve. He sent two. Plus, he sent them secretly. He was not going to have a repeat of what happened a generation earlier when ten of twelve spies went south really quickly in their public report. This pair of spies was to focus their attention on getting actionable intel on the great walled city of Jericho.

So the spies made their way up to the city, slipped past the gates, and looked around at the fortifications and defenses. Trying to blend in, the spies chose to stay at Rahab the prostitute's home, which was a risky but strategic place to gather information (v. 1). But in the process, their presence in Jericho was discovered. In fact, the king sent his men to Rahab, demanding that she turn them over (vv. 2–3). Obviously, ancient Near-Eastern cultures placed a high value on hospitality, which included not only caring for guests but protecting them if necessary. Yet Rahab went above and beyond mere hospitality by putting her own life on the line for these foreign Hebrew intruders. What courage Rahab demonstrated by showing the spies mercy, hiding them, and sending the king's soldiers off on a wild goose chase so the Hebrew spies could lay low then eventually escape (vv. 4–7)! Obviously, she lied in order to protect them, for which the biblical writer neither excuses or praises her. Once the coast was clear, Rahab approached the spies with a proposition in verses 9–13:

> "I know that the Lord has given you the land, that the terror of you has fallen on us, and that all the inhabitants of the land are fainthearted because of you. For we have heard how the Lord dried up the water of the Red Sea for you when you came out of Egypt, and what you did to the two kings of the Amorites who were on the other side of the Jordan, Sihon and Og, whom you utterly destroyed. And

> as soon as we heard these things, our hearts melted; neither did there remain any more courage in anyone because of you, for the LORD your God, He is God in heaven above and on earth beneath. Now therefore, I beg you, swear to me by the LORD, since I have shown you kindness, that you also will show kindness to my father's house, and give me a true token, and spare my father, my mother, my brothers, my sisters, and all that they have, and deliver our lives from death."

Isn't this amazing? This pagan prostitute had not only heard about how the Hebrew God Yahweh miraculously divided the Red Sea and given the children of Israel victory over seemingly invincible enemies; Rahab had also believed: "the LORD your God, He is God in heaven above and on earth beneath" (v. 11). This surprising statement of faith shows that God was not only at work in her heart but also had a plan in bringing Rahab and the spies together.

As we continue to read, the spies agreed to Rahab's terms and escaped (vv. 14–21). When they made their way back to home base, they reported to Joshua: "Truly the LORD has delivered all the land into our hands, for indeed all the inhabitants of the country are fainthearted because of us" (v. 24; see also v. 9). By the way, this is the "dread and fear" their enemies would experience just as God had promised back in Deuteronomy 2:25. Through their obedience, God's promise had come to fruition. And through that, the world saw the power and the majesty of God.

When we take a step back and think about the story of Rahab, it serves as a powerful illustration of the life-transforming power of God. Here's Rahab, a well-known prostitute in Jericho, a person living in spiritual darkness and depravity, yet her story is one of amazing grace. Despite her idolatry and immorality, Rahab's encounter with the Hebrew spies Joshua sent and, more importantly, her encounter with the God of the Hebrews led to a profound change in the trajectory of her life. Her transformation became so complete that she is later commended in the New Testament as an example of faith proven by her works (Heb. 11:31; James 2:25).

Rahab's conversion underscores another significant truth: God's presence at work in the lives of His people can lead to conviction and transformation in others. In fact, the presence of God in our lives ought to be so evident that it raises questions among nonbelievers, leading them to seek God and ultimately surrender their lives to Him. We see this occur in the book of Acts. Remember when the early Christians in Acts 2 were filled with the Holy Spirit on the day of Pentecost? When onlookers from all over the world heard these mostly Galilean disciples speaking in their own languages and dialects, the spectacle caused the crowd to be amazed and perplexed, asking what was happening and what it meant. Then Peter preached a Spirit-filled message, and in response, they asked what they needed to do to be saved. It was the same with the Philippian jailer in Acts 16, when he heard Paul and Silas praying and singing praises to God in the dungeon. God sent an earthquake, and the jailer eventually asked the same question. The question we need to ask is whether those who encounter us also encounter our God in His power and glory.

The reality of God's providence is also highlighted in Joshua 2, showing us how God orchestrates events and encounters to fulfill His divine plan. Just as God providentially guided the Hebrew spies to seek refuge with none other than Rahab, the prostitute, God is actively involved in guiding believers to those whose hearts have been prepared to receive the message of Christ. We learn from the New Testament that the Holy Spirit works in the hearts of nonbelievers to convict them of sin, righteousness, and judgment (John 16:8), while simultaneously empowering believers to witness and share the gospel (Acts 1:8). This dual action of the Holy Spirit is essential for God's work of bringing people to faith in Christ. Yes, it begins in the heart of the person who needs Jesus, but it continues with God providentially orchestrating the meeting with those of us who know and follow Him. We should keep our spiritual eyes open for those divine appointments and make the most of the opportunities God puts before us to make a difference in the lives of the people He puts in our paths.

This brings up yet another truth here for us to apply: God values our availability to serve His purposes more than our abilities. When we offer ourselves as willing vessels, God can use us to make a positive impact on others. This perspective shifts the focus from our own talents to God's power working through us. Paul puts it this way in 2 Corinthians 4:7: "But we have this treasure in earthen vessels, that the excellence of the power may be of God and not of us." Live a life visibly transformed by God's power, which in turn can lead others to inquire about the faith and ultimately find salvation through Christ. So be ready and willing to be used by God to reach others with the gospel. God values our availability.

Rahab ultimately married Salmon, whom some conjecture was one of the Hebrew spies she sheltered. What is certain is that she gave birth to Boaz, the great-grandfather of King David. Her name is included in the genealogy of Jesus in the Gospel of Matthew (1:5). Consequently, the story of Rahab is a powerful illustration of the gospel, demonstrating that no one is beyond the reach of God's saving grace. Her transformation from a life of sin to a place of honor within the lineage of Jesus Christ proves the profound change God can bring about in a person's life and offers hope for all. Is there someone you know who seems far from God's grace? How can you pray for them and show them the love of Christ, believing in their potential for becoming an example of God's transforming grace? The story of Rahab confirms that anyone can be redeemed and used by God for His glory.

Questions for Reflection and Discussion

1. What specifically caused the hearts of the people of Jericho to melt in fear before the Israelites crossed the Jordan River?
2. What did Rahab ask in payment for sheltering the Hebrew spies?
   a. Five gold coins
   b. A five-star review
   c. The lives of her family when the Hebrews took Jericho
   d. None of the above

Notes on Today's Bible Reading

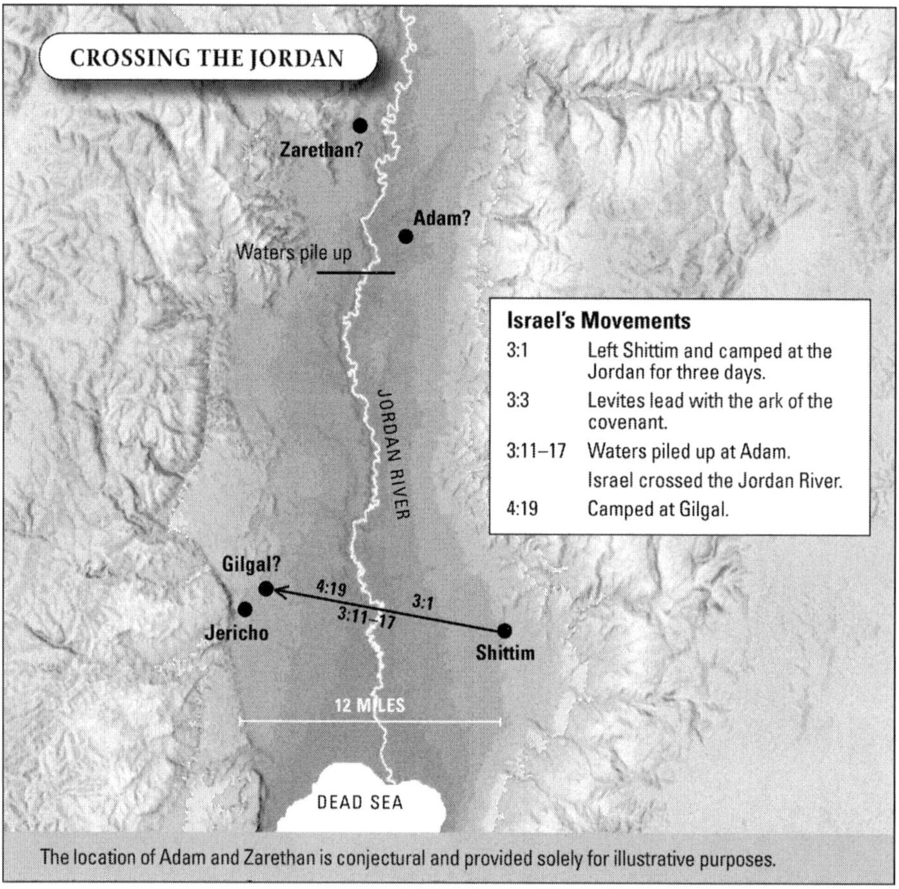

Map courtesy of The Readable Bible (www.readablebible.com)

— Day 4 —

Today's Reading: Joshua 3

Verse of the Day

> And Joshua said to the people, "Sanctify yourselves, for tomorrow the LORD will do wonders among you."
>
> *Joshua 3:5*

Please read the entire Scripture selection in your own Bible and highlight or underline verses that stand out to you before you read the observations and engage the questions below.

Today we are in Joshua 3. In this chapter, we witness one of the mighty miracles in the Old Testament. God told Joshua to have the priests lead the people down to the Jordan River, which was a rushing torrent. Picture how this played out. The priests carried the ark of the covenant, which represented God's presence among His people, and marched out in front of the people, taking that gold-covered ark right into the edge of the raging river. And God rolled that river back when the feet of the priests touched the waters, and then they walked out to the middle of the riverbed. What an unforgettable experience it must have been for the Israelites! Not only did they see the waters flee from under their feet, but they also watched the big mountain of water hovering and pulsating above their heads, growing higher with every passing minute. Yet

God miraculously held back the river, so they could pass over on dry ground. And out of this remarkable encounter with almighty God in Joshua 3, several high points are worth noting and considering.[2]

First, notice before God moved miraculously, the people were *sanctified.* Look at 3:5: "And Joshua said to the people, 'Sanctify yourselves, for tomorrow the LORD will do wonders among you.'" In the process of preparing to cross the river, there was a rededication, a revival of sorts. The idea is they were to pray, confess sin, and ask for forgiveness and cleansing. That's what it means when Joshua asked them to sanctify or consecrate themselves. They were to be spiritually prepared for what God wanted them to do next. Go back and look at the history of Israel, and even in early America, and how great moves of God were preceded by an acute awareness of sinfulness and heart-felt repentance. God brings us to a moment that is so vital, so critical, so important, it calls for spiritual preparation, sanctification, cleansing—a return to holiness. Remember that. If we hope to see God move, we must do the same. The people were sanctified.

Second, the word of God was *verified.* In the first part of chapter 3, God essentially told Joshua, "Tell the priests to carry the ark down into the waters of the Jordan, and when they do, you'll see the miracle." So the people of God took Joshua at his word because Joshua had taken God at His word:

> [A]nd as those who bore the ark came to the Jordan, and the feet of the priests who bore the ark dipped in the edge of the water (for the Jordan overflows all its banks during the whole time of harvest), that the waters which came down from upstream stood still, and rose in a heap very far away at Adam, the city that is beside Zaretan. So the waters

> that went down into the Sea of the Arabah, the Salt Sea, failed, and were cut off; and the people crossed over opposite Jericho. (3:15–16)

God did exactly what He told Joshua He was going to do. When the priests stepped in the water, God stopped the raging river and the people crossed on dry ground. Consequently, God's word was verified. You see, Joshua taught the Israelites to trust God. He believed God's promises and knew he had to instruct the people in the imperative to rely on God, not on men or horses and chariots. God keeps His word. Remember that.

Third, Joshua was *magnified*. God told Joshua, "This day I will begin to exalt you in the sight of all Israel, that they may know that, as I was with Moses, so I will be with you" (v. 7). Remember, Joshua was given the awesome assignment of being Moses' successor, and no doubt Joshua was a little intimidated by that because God had to keep telling him in the first chapter, "Be strong and very courageous." And essentially, God told him, "Joshua, now that you're the leader, I'm going to do something so awesome through you that they will follow you like they followed Moses. I'm going to magnify you before the people." Did that happen? Look at 4:14: "On that day the Lord exalted Joshua in the sight of all Israel; and they feared him, as they had feared Moses, all the days of his life." The word translated "feared" in this case means revered or held in awe, but the point is, it happened just as God said. So the people were sanctified, God's word was verified, and Joshua was magnified.

Fourth, God was *glorified*. Joshua pointed to the miracle God worked at the Jordan and proclaimed, "By this you shall know that the living God is among you" (v. 10a). Word got out about God delivering His people out of Egypt and bringing them to this land.

Remember Rahab said, "I know that the Lord has given you the land, that the terror of you has fallen on us, and that all the inhabitants of the land are fainthearted because of you. For we have heard how the Lord dried up the water of the Red Sea for you when you came out of Egypt, and what you did to the two kings of the Amorites . . . whom you utterly destroyed" (2:9–10). Indeed, as we read in chapter 4, Joshua had the people set up memorials to this miracle so "that all the peoples of the earth may know the hand of the Lord, that it is mighty" (v. 24). News spread all over Canaan, and wherever people met, they talked about the great God of Israel (5:1). So the people were sanctified, the word of God was verified, Joshua was magnified, and God was glorified. Remember that. God's miraculous deeds should inspire us to bring Him glory.

Think about it. The priests had to stand with the ark on their shoulders while all of the children of Israel walked around them and then on to the other side. At any moment, if God had released it, that mountain of water would have come crashing down and swept them all away. But those priests stayed right in the middle of the riverbed until the last Israelite had "passed clean over" (3:17 KJV). All the people must have passed by the wall of water in awe. But for those priests to stand there in the riverbed and for those people to cross over were demonstrations of real faith!

This new generation of Israelites may not have witnessed the miraculous deliverance from Egypt. They may have been too young to recall the spectacle of the Red Sea divided. Consequently, they needed this faith-building experience with God at the Jordan to prepare them for the battles ahead. Look at how Joshua framed it in verse 10: "By this you shall know that the living God is among you, and that He will without fail drive out from before you the Canaanites and the Hittites and the Hivites and the Perizzites and the Girgashites and the Amorites and the Jebusites." Sometimes God wants us to stand in the middle of an impossible-looking situation while a mountain of threatening circumstances builds higher and higher so that we learn to trust him more deeply. Then when God delivers us, our faith is strengthened for the next assignment and challenge. At the same time, when God makes a way where there is no way, it should prompt us to praise Him and give Him glory.

Questions for Reflection and Discussion

1. What did Joshua command the people to do in preparation for God working a mighty miracle?
    a. Pack your bags and get a good night's rest
    b. Have your phones charged and cameras ready
    c. Sanctify or consecrate yourselves
    d. None of the above

2. How did the people view Joshua after God stopped the flooding Jordan River and the people crossed into the promised land?

Notes on Today's Bible Reading

— Day 5 —

Today's Reading: Joshua 4

Verse of the Day

> Then Joshua set up twelve stones in the midst of the Jordan, in the place where the feet of the priests who bore the ark of the covenant stood; and they are there to this day.
>
> *Joshua 4:9*

Please read the entire Scripture selection in your own Bible and highlight or underline verses that stand out to you before you read the observations and engage the questions below.

Today we are in Joshua 4. In this chapter, God instructed Joshua to have the people commemorate the awesome miracle at the Jordan River with two stone monuments. The memorials were teaching tools to remind future generations never to fret over what is in the future when God is with them. And again, for us, the God who guides us will also provide and make a way where there is no way. From Joshua 4, we learn God wants His people to always remember what He did for them on that day. The stacks of stones would be used as spiritual markers to help people recall how God miraculously stopped the Jordan River at its flood stage.

In fact, we are told Joshua built one himself in the dry riverbed (v. 9). Some might ask, "What good is a monument in the middle of the Jordan after the waters returned and covered them?" Well, the river at this point was at flood stage, but it didn't stay that way. When the waters of the Jordan receded during the late spring and summer, right at the spot where the people crossed over and where the priests had stood, this monument of stones appeared as a visible reminder that God had been faithful. Then Joshua built another stone monument at their camp, which they called Gilgal (v. 20). God had providentially, supernaturally, and miraculously intervened, and they were to set up stone monuments to help them remember what God did for them.

All throughout Scripture, God established memorials to remind His people of their experiences with Him. After God had safely delivered Noah and his family from the flood, God put a memorial in the sky in the form of a rainbow. God gave Abraham the sign of circumcision to separate the Hebrews from all the peoples around them. God gave the Hebrews the Passover as a meal to commemorate their deliverance from Egypt. Even the ark of the covenant and its contents served as a memorial. Do you remember what was in it? Aaron's rod that budded, a golden urn filled with manna, and the two tablets of the Ten Commandments—all reminders of their sojourn in the wilderness and God's gracious provision. God loves memorials. Why did the Lord institute all these memorials, which were physical markers of God's providence? Because we tend to forget what God has done. Moses had recently warned the people of Israel about the danger of forgetting in Deuteronomy 8:11–20. To guard against this, many of God's people recognized the value of erecting memorials as a way of remembering or marking their experiences with God. Abraham, Isaac, and Jacob built stone altars as a reminder of God's providence, provision, and presence, and they often gave these places names. Jacob named the place where he met with God "Bethel," meaning "the house of God." Moses named the place where they defeated the Amorites "The Lord is my Banner." Samuel named a stone "Ebenezer," saying, "Thus far the Lord helped us." Here are some principles to remember about these memorials.

First, memorials *encourage* the present generation. Many times we think memorials are only for the future, and they are for the future, but they are also a powerful faith-building tool in the present. Memorials encourage the present generation. Look at Joshua 4:19–20: "Now the people came up from the Jordan on the tenth day of the first month, and they camped in Gilgal on the east border of Jericho. And those twelve stones which they took out of the Jordan, Joshua set up in Gilgal." Think about all of the times the Israelites went into battle—there were certainly times when they were discouraged from losing. But when they came back to the camp at Gilgal, all they had to do was look over at that stone monument Joshua had built to the glory of their great God. The monument of stones from the midst of the Jordan was a silent but visible witness to the fact their God had rolled back the river so they could walk over on dry ground. No doubt they came in and looked at the memorial and said, "What a mighty God we serve!"

Second, memorials *educate* the next generation. God wants us to use memorials as a teaching tool. Each of us needs to do our part in teaching the next generation about the memorials and even the monuments that reflect God's sovereignty, faithfulness, and omnipresence. Joshua explained the purpose for this memorial in verses 6–7: "that this may be a sign among you when your children ask in time to come, saying, 'What do these stones mean to you?' Then you shall answer them that the waters of the Jordan were cut off before the ark of the covenant of the Lord; when it crossed over the Jordan, the waters of the Jordan were cut off. And these stones shall be for a memorial to the children of Israel forever."

Then again in verses 21–23: "When your children ask their fathers in time to come, saying, 'What are these stones?' then you shall let your children know, saying, 'Israel crossed over this Jordan on dry land'; for the LORD your God dried up the waters of the Jordan before you until you had crossed over, as the Lord your God did to the Red Sea, which He dried up before us until we had crossed over.'" See, our children need to be reminded of their spiritual heritage, and Joshua pictured a time when the children of the people who crossed over would come to their fathers and mothers and say, "Hey, Mom and Dad, I was walking around in Gilgal and saw this big pile of stones. What do they mean?" Joshua said, "Sit down with your kids and say: 'Let me tell you what those stones mean. You know there was a day when we were on the other side of the raging river Jordan and it was flooding its banks, and there was no way across. But kids, we trusted God, walked toward that river and as soon as the priests stepped in, the river rolled back and we walked over on dry ground! Kids, that's the kind of mighty God we serve. He's our God!" Memorials educate the next generation.

Just as Joshua put up a stone monument as a testimony, my family and I have what we call a Joshua basket. It's filled with rocks, and on each of those rocks, we write a number. Then, in a journal that accompanies the basket of rocks, there is a corresponding entry for each numbered rock. There we write about the faithfulness of God, of how He answered a prayer or how He saw us through a situation, something we were praying for. See, there will come a time when we're not here as parents, as fathers. But if the Lord takes me home tomorrow, I want my children to be able to go back to that basket, take out a rock, and read of God's faithfulness. I want my grandchildren and great-grandchildren to read of His faithfulness in that journal. We need to be intentional about instructing our children about the greatness and glory of God. If not, they will be led astray by the culture to follow the gods of this age. And we see this repeated over and over to the children of Israel, especially as they're crossing into the promised land.

Finally, memorials not only encourage the present generation and educate the next generation, but they also provide a lasting witness as *evidence* to a watching world of the might of the true and living God. Look at verse 24a: "that all the peoples of the earth may know the hand of the LORD, that it is mighty." Remember how God's mighty acts of dividing the Red Sea and defeating the Amorite kings convinced Rahab (2:8–11)? That's another reason God told Israel, "I want you to build these memorials in the midst of the river, and in the midst of the camp at Gilgal because I want the people of the nations to look at those stones and know that I am the true and living God." God wants us to set up memorials to encourage the present generation, educate our children, and present as evidence to a watching world that our God is the only true God. Now, obviously, God doesn't want us to necessarily stack stones everywhere we have an experience with Him, but He does want us to somehow memorialize these encounters and relate them to our children and grandchildren as well as to a watching world that our God is the true and living God. Joshua closes out this chapter with a concluding thought on these memorials and their purpose: "that you may fear the LORD your God forever" (v. 24b). What a great reminder for us!

Questions for Reflection and Discussion

1. After God stopped the raging waters of the Jordan River so that the people could cross on dry ground, why did He command a stone monument be built?

2. What was the message to the "peoples of the earth" behind the monument?
   a. That the God of the Hebrews is a god of stone
   b. That the God of the Hebrews requires a stone offering
   c. That the God of the Hebrews is mighty
   d. None of the above

Notes on Today's Bible Reading

— Day 6 —

Today's Reading: Joshua 5

Verse of the Day

> So He said, "No, but as Commander of the army of the LORD I have now come."
>
> And Joshua fell on his face to the earth and worshiped, and said to Him, "What does my Lord say to His servant?"
>
> *Joshua 5:14*

Please read the entire Scripture selection in your own Bible and highlight or underline verses that stand out to you before you read the observations and engage the questions below.

Today we are in Joshua 5. In this chapter, the people of God firmly reestablished their identity before going into their first battle against the residents of the walled city of Jericho. By this point, God had already miraculously stopped the raging river Jordan so Israel could cross. Now they were preparing for the military campaigns to defeat the hostile inhabitants of the land. For those of you who have served in combat, this chapter might seem to be a strange way of preparing to go to war, especially from a man's point of view. From all human appearances, this was the time to attack. God had given to Joshua, and Joshua had given to the people God's promises of success and victory if they followed the direction of His word handed down through Moses. The people of Israel were no doubt filled with confidence after miraculously crossing the Jordan River on dry ground. Plus, intelligence reports came in that the enemy was demoralized and in disarray (5:1). Surely, it was time to launch the offensive. No doubt Joshua's tribal commanders must have been thinking, *It is "go time" Joshua. The enemy is scared and shaking in his sandals. Let's do this!* Yet God's ways are higher than our ways. God basically said, "First things first. Follow the direction of my word!" To ensure victory, God required two observances from the law that reestablished their identity: submitting to circumcision and observing the Passover.

Submitting to Circumcision (5:2–9)

The focus on circumcision in Scripture may seem a bit odd, but it was a regular reminder of submission to the Lord of creation. Verse 2: "At that time, the Lord said to Joshua, 'Make flint knives for yourself, and circumcise the sons of Israel again the second time.'" Yet verse 3 tells us the men of Israel stepped forward and took a radical step of obedience to be identified as God's people in a painful and permanent way. Obviously, when God said, "circumcise the sons of Israel a second time," He did not mean the men who had already been circumcised were to be circumcised a second time. The only two guys living who had gone through the ordeal already were Joshua and Caleb. It happened back in Egypt right before they were about to leave in the exodus. In fact, Egyptians practiced circumcision as a religious ritual reserved for the priests and the upper class. So, it was likely prohibited as a practice for the Israelites. But then on the eve of the exodus, every male who ate the Passover in Egypt, native Israelite or stranger, was then circumcised (see Exod. 12:43–49). Fast forward some forty years later and God was requiring it of this new generation who came out of the wilderness and were poised to take the promised land.

But why the renewal of the rite of circumcision and especially now? I mean, let's be real. Performing crude circumcision with stone knives on grown men would certainly leave the men of war vulnerable to attack because it totally incapacitated them for a while. In fact, a similar scenario actually played out in Genesis 34 when Simeon and Levi tricked the men of Shechem into being circumcised then killed them when they were convalescing. Again, why delay the attack on Jericho for this religious rite? Joshua 5:4–9 explains:

> And this is the reason why Joshua circumcised them: All the people who came out of Egypt who were males, all the men of war, had died in the wilderness on the way, after they had come out of Egypt. For all the people who came out had been circumcised, but all the people born in the wilderness, on the way as they came out of Egypt, had not been circumcised. For the children of Israel walked forty years in the wilderness, till all the people who were men of war, who came out of Egypt, were consumed, because they did not obey the voice of the Lord—to whom the Lord swore that He would not show them the land which the Lord had sworn to their fathers that He would give us, "a land flowing with milk and honey." Then Joshua circumcised their sons whom He raised up in their place; for they were uncircumcised, because they had not been circumcised on the way. So it was, when they had finished circumcising all the people, that they stayed in their places in the camp till they were healed. Then the Lord said to Joshua, "This

day I have rolled away the reproach of Egypt from you." Therefore the name of the place is called Gilgal to this day.

First of all, circumcision was about reestablishing their identity as God's peculiar people. It was a permanent sign of the covenant promises of God to Abraham and to his descendants. It was therefore the means of becoming physically identified with the people of God for a male Israelite. Consequently, no uncircumcised male could legitimately partake of the Passover (Exod. 12:43–44). The Passover reminded them of God's deliverance of Israel from Egyptian bondage. Yet the deliverance had as its goal the possession of this land.

That leads to the second reason for this mass circumcision: None of the men born during their wilderness wanderings had been circumcised (Josh. 5:4–7). Lack of circumcision during those forty years was either further evidence of their faithless disobedience or more likely it was because they were unfit as a people under judgment to be circumcised. Remember, the sentence handed down by God in Numbers 14:26–35 was that none of the men aged twenty and older would be allowed to enter the promised land (except for Joshua and Caleb) because they did not trust God to give them victory over the people of the land. Instead, they had rebelled, and God judged them. Circumcision was a sign of God's covenant with Abraham and his descendants, which included the promised land as a possession (see Gen. 17:8–9). Consequently, that rebellious generation under God's judgment could never possess the land, so that may be why they were uncircumcised.

This brings us to the third reason: The new generation had to receive circumcision as a sign of the covenant before possessing the land God promised them. In fact, the Lord acknowledged the completion of circumcision with the words, "This day I have rolled away the reproach of Egypt from you" (Josh. 5:9). The Hebrew word used for "roll away" is from the same root for the place named "Gilgal," which means a circle and referred to the circle of stones placed at Gilgal when they were crossing the Jordan as a memorial of God's deliverance. The word for "wheel" comes from this word. So there is a play on words here for the sake of teaching an important truth.

Through the cutting away of the foreskin, circumcision symbolized the "rolling away" of the "reproach of Egypt." What was this disgrace? Naysaying Egyptians apparently mocked Israel for wandering aimlessly in the wilderness for forty years, concluding that Israel's God had abandoned them. Moses predicted Egypt would do this if God actually had followed through in the threat to destroy them in response to their faithless rebellion (Exod. 32:12; Num. 14:13–16; Deut. 9:28). This new generation was at the same moment of decision as the previous generation was in Numbers 14, poised to take the land. The rebellious generation disbelieved and disobeyed God and died in the wilderness. This new generation trusted and obeyed God and therefore would possess the land. So circumcision was an act of consecration necessary before possessing the promised land.

Observing the Passover (5:10)

With circumcision accomplished, the people were spiritually ready and qualified to observe the Passover. It is also providential that they crossed just in time to observe it on the fourteenth day of the month. God's timing is perfect. This was only the third Passover the people had kept. The first was in Egypt (Exod. 12:1–28), the second was at Mount Sinai just before they broke camp to head toward the promised land (Num. 9:1–5) and then went on a forty-year detour, and the third time was here at Gilgal. Why the Passover? To relive their deliverance out of Egypt by the blood of the Lamb sprinkled on the entries of their homes. Celebrating the Passover not only reminded them of their deliverance and redemption out of Egypt, but it looked forward to other victories, such as to the conquest of all the enemies entrenched in the promised land, and also to an ultimate victory over the enemy of our souls accomplished on Calvary. Passover naturally pointed to the cross where "Christ, our Passover, was sacrificed for us" (1 Cor. 5:7b).

Now that we are talking New Testament truths, circumcision has its parallel in baptism for the follower of Jesus. But baptism pictures the death, burial, and resurrection of Christ. Obviously, the Passover has its New Testament parallel in the Lord's Supper or Communion. The supper is the memorial meal where we are to remember the person and work of Christ who was sacrificed as the Lamb of God who took our place and our punishment, bearing our sin that we might have life, abundant and eternal. As the rite of circumcision and Passover observance were to an Israelite, so baptism and the Lord's Supper are to a New Testament follower of Christ. Again, they identify us as belonging to Christ.

We identify with so many rival tribes today. It starts early with sports teams and schools, then it graduates to brands like Apple or Android, Coke or Pepsi, Ford or Chevy, Smith & Wesson or Sig Sauer, then eventually to political parties like Democrat or Republican. In fact, people sport a lot of different "team jerseys," finding their identity in their ethnic group, sexual preferences, economic philosophy, or whatever. Some are good, some neutral; others are harmful, even sinful. Yet the most important "jersey" of all is the one that identifies us as a follower of Jesus Christ.

By submitting to circumcision and partaking of the Passover, the people of Israel were renewing their covenant with God. When they did, God said their reproach was rolled away, their identity was changed. They were no longer slaves from Egypt, no longer wilderness wanderers, but now children of God ready to take possession of the promised land. When we fully embrace our identity in Christ Jesus, the reproach of the past, the bondage of sin, the things that we have done, are rolled away. This is what provides our children with their identity and abundant life as they enter into a relationship with the Lord Jesus Christ. And that's up to us as parents and grandparents to continually keep this before our children and, quite frankly, in a broader sense, to fight to make sure this is kept in our culture and that believers, followers of Jesus Christ, can freely live and speak openly about their faith.

Joshua 5 concludes with Joshua's dramatic encounter with the Commander of the army of the Lord with his sword drawn (vv. 13–15). In fact, God had declared back in Exodus: "Behold, I send an angel before you to guard you on the way and to bring you to the place that I have prepared" (23:20). When Joshua asked if He was for them or for their enemies, the heavenly Warrior basically said, "Neither." In other words, "I'm not on your side or their side; I've not come to take sides; I've come to take over!" How we need to hear this today. God hasn't come to take sides; He has come to take over. Listen, if you want victory in your life, stop trying to get God on your side. Get on God's side! Stop trying to get Him to "bless your mess." Let Him take over. Hit the restart with the Lord in the lead. You will never know victory, and your Jericho will never fall until you do as Joshua did and lay your sword down and bow down before Him. And when you do that, Jericho is no longer your problem; it becomes God's problem, and for God it is no problem at all.

That makes all the difference in the world, doesn't it? When you can turn over your Jericho to the One who has come to take over.

Questions for Reflection and Discussion

1.Why did God require the males to be circumcised?

2. What was Joshua's response to the Commander of the Lord's army?

Notes on Today's Bible Reading

— Day 7 —

Today's Reading: Joshua 6

Verse of the Day

> And the LORD said to Joshua: "See! I have given Jericho into your hand, its king, and the mighty men of valor."
>
> *Joshua 6:2*

Please read the entire Scripture selection in your own Bible and highlight or underline verses that stand out to you before you read the observations and engage the questions below.

Today we are in Joshua 6. In this chapter, we read about the battle of Jericho, which was really no battle at all when "the walls came a-tumblin' down." Remember, the children of Israel had done everything God asked in preparation for this battle. They had sanctified themselves, the males had submitted to circumcision, and they had celebrated the Passover—the first time in forty years. This new generation renewed the covenant with Yahweh God. At the same time, manna stopped falling from heaven, and they started living off the produce of the promised land.

And as we read at the end of chapter 5, Joshua had the dramatic encounter with the Commander of the army of the Lord (5:13–15). Recall that Joshua laid his sword at the feet of this sword-wielding heavenly Warrior and bowed down to the ground in reverence. And the Commander said, "Take your sandal off your foot, for the place where you stand is holy." And Joshua took off his sandals. Remember this happening before? At the burning bush? God spoke to Moses essentially these same words in Exodus 3:5.

Joshua was dealing with the God of angel armies, but why did God make Himself known to Joshua at this strategic moment? Apparently, He had come to give Joshua the plan to take Jericho. As we see in chapter 6, it is a plan so unconventional, so improbable, that when it was executed both Israel and the nations knew that God alone had accomplished it.

Let's begin in Joshua 6:2: "And the LORD said to Joshua: 'See! I have given Jericho into your hand, its king, and the mighty men of valor.'" Jericho was a strategic city because it was located pretty much in the middle of Canaan. It was on the right—on the eastern portion of the land of Canaan as one crossed over the Jordan. From a strategic standpoint, taking Jericho divided the land north and south and made it more difficult for the kingdoms of the north and the south to join forces against Israel. By the way, this is a strategy many military leaders have used in their conquests throughout the ages. In fact, this is exactly what Russia did in their attempt to take Ukraine. They attacked the capital city, Kiev, which is in the middle of the country, dividing the country from west to east. The point is that Jericho was a strategic city.

Jericho was also a formidable city with its double wall defenses surrounding it. From a human perspective, it seemed as if there was no way Joshua and the Hebrews could take it. It was an impossible-looking situation. There's an old chorus that runs, "Got any rivers you think are uncrossable? Got any mountains you can't tunnel through? God specializes in things tho't impossible. He does the things others cannot do."[3] God loves to tackle things that look impossible, to demonstrate His mighty power and bring glory to Himself.

Let's move on to Joshua 6:3–5.

> "You shall march around the city, all you men of war; you shall go all around the city once. This you shall do six days. And seven priests shall bear seven trumpets of rams' horns before the ark. But the seventh day you shall march around the city seven times, and the priests shall blow the trumpets. It shall come to pass, when they make a long blast with the ram's horn, and when you hear the sound of the trumpet, that all the people shall shout with a great shout; then the wall of the city will fall down flat. And the people shall go up every man straight before him."

Can you imagine getting these orders? What was required of those who executed this plan? Faith—*a lot* of faith.

Hold this thought, and let's see what happened. Look down at verses 20–21: "So the people shouted when the priests blew the trumpets. And it happened when the people heard the sound of the trumpet, and the people shouted with a great shout, that the wall fell down flat. Then the people went up into the city, every man straight before him, and they took the city. And they utterly destroyed all that was in the city, both man and woman, young and old, ox and sheep and donkey, with the edge of the sword." But one caveat here: Joshua and his armies honored the agreement struck with Rahab back in chapter 2: "But Joshua had said to the two men who had spied out the country, 'Go into the harlot's house, and from there bring out the woman and all that she has, as you swore to her'" (6:22). Then we have this postscript in verse 25: "And

Joshua spared Rahab the harlot, her father's household, and all that she had. So she dwells in Israel to this day, because she hid the messengers whom Joshua sent to spy out Jericho."

OK, so let's go back and ask the question: Why did God give this unconventional plan to Joshua and the people of Israel? He was putting their faith to the test—but especially the faith of Joshua. God doesn't tell Joshua to build battering rams or siegeworks or ladders. Instead, He tells Joshua to do something that from the human perspective seemed silly: (1) March around the walls (round and round you go, where you stop nobody knows); (2) blow your trumpets; (3) shout! That's no military strategy. Everybody knows that won't work. You can't take a city that way. It just can't be done. Except it did! What did the children of Israel have to do? Simply trust and obey. Hebrews 11:30 gives us the postscript on the battle of Jericho: "By faith the walls of Jericho fell down after they were encircled for seven days." How did God enable the children of Israel to do the impossible? By faith!

Yet what a test of faith this plan must have been for Joshua! Slip into his sandals for a moment. As I mentioned previously, Joshua was a trained military leader, and he was not being instructed by the Lord to attack with troops but with trumpets, not with siege works but with a shout. This made no sense. Joshua would look foolish in the eyes of the Israelites if this did not work out, and it would also make the startup nation look like a bunch of clowns in the eyes of the Canaanites. But why did God choose to have Joshua and the Israelites do it this way? Well, look at 6:27: "So the LORD was with Joshua, and his fame spread throughout all the country." The destruction of Jericho and the unconventional way it happened only magnified the fear of those who heard about it. And as Joshua humbled himself before the Lord in obedience, God lifted him up in a significant way, both in the eyes of the children of Israel and in the surrounding nations. At times God will call us to do things in unconventional ways. Almost everything in the kingdom of God is counterintuitive, and it takes faith and obedience to step out. And oftentimes, that first step is the one that seems the most illogical in the eyes of the world. So we have to get out of our worldly mindset and think in terms of the kingdom of God.

Questions for Reflection and Discussion

1. On the seventh day when the people of Israel blew trumpets and shouted, what happened in Jericho?
   a. Officials issued citations for breaking the city noise ordinance.
   b. The walls fell flat.
   c. The windows rattled.
   d. None of the above

2. Everyone in Jericho was killed except for whose family?

Notes on Today's Bible Reading

— Day 8 —

Today's Reading: Joshua 7–8

Verse of the Day

> "Get up, sanctify the people, and say, 'Sanctify yourselves for tomorrow, because thus says the LORD God of Israel: "There is an accursed thing in your midst, O Israel; you cannot stand before your enemies until you take away the accursed thing from among you."'"
>
> *Joshua 7:13*

Please read the entire Scripture selection in your own Bible and highlight or underline verses that stand out to you before you read the observations and engage the questions below.

Today we are in Joshua 7–8, but before we dive into chapter 7, let's look at the instructions given about the actual attack on Jericho in chapter 6. These specific instructions have huge implications for chapter 7. Look at Joshua 6:18–19: "'And you, by all means abstain from the accursed things, lest you become accursed when you take of the accursed things and make the camp of Israel a curse and trouble it. But all the silver and gold, and vessels of bronze and iron, are consecrated to the LORD; they shall come into the treasury of the LORD.'" They were not to take anything. They were told to destroy everything. Any of the silver and the gold and those precious metals were going to be dedicated to the temple. Of course, they had to burn them and consecrate them for the tabernacle. The people were to keep nothing.

Let's look at this familiar story of Achan beginning in Joshua 7:1: "But the children of Israel committed a trespass regarding the accursed things, for Achan the son of Carmi, the son of Zabdi, the son of Zerah, of the tribe of Judah, took of the accursed things; so the anger of the LORD burned against the children of Israel." Then we see that the sin of one was accounted to all: "'Israel has sinned, and they have also transgressed My covenant which I commanded them. For they have even taken some of the accursed things, and have both stolen and deceived; and they have also put it among their own stuff'" (v. 11). Only one guy did it—Achan—yet with this hidden trespass, they were all held accountable.

They then mounted an attack on Ai with a small force, and we read about that in verses 4 and 5: "So about three thousand men went up there from the people, but they fled before the men of Ai. And the men of Ai struck down about thirty-six men, for they chased them from before the gate as far as Shebarim, and struck them down on the descent; therefore, the hearts of the people melted and became like water." We see the sin of one affects many. That's why we can't ignore what's happening around us. Burying our heads in the sand is not going to protect us.

Before we move on, it is important to note that Achan's sin wasn't the only one committed here. Pastor Adrian Rogers pointed out three.[4] First, there is sin of pride. Joshua again sent spies, but they came back with this report: "'Do not let all the people go up, but let about two or three thousand men go up and attack Ai. Do not weary all the people there, for the people of Ai are few'" (v. 3). Maybe they said to themselves, "If we can take Jericho, Ai will be a piece of cake. So, no need to send out the entire army on this mission." But they forgot that Jericho ultimately wasn't their victory. It was God's victory. So there was pride. Second, the child of pride is presumption. They expected to win. They thought, *We did it before; we'll do it again.* Consequently, they sent in only a fraction of their military force to take Ai, and yet they were soundly defeated. They presumed on God for victory. Third, there was the sin of prayerlessness. Not once do we read that Joshua sought the Lord about Ai before attacking it. As we see in the following verses, he did pray after they got in trouble, and he prayed a whole lot. That's like so many believers who launch out without praying, make a mess, then ask God to fix it.

We see his prayer beginning in verse 7: "And Joshua said, 'Alas, Lord God, why have You brought this people over the Jordan at all—to deliver us into the hand of the Amorites, to destroy us? Oh, that we had been content, and dwelt on the other side of the Jordan!'" The effects of sin are demoralizing. Here, what had occurred demoralized the leader. He still did not know what Achan had done, but this defeat, which was the consequence of sin, was demoralizing. He continued in verses 8–9: "'O Lord, what shall I say when Israel turns its back before its enemies? For the Canaanites and all the inhabitants of land will hear it, and surround us, and cut off our name from the earth. Then what will You do for Your great name?'"

The effects of sin not only bring a demoralizing effect upon us, but they bring reproach upon the name of the Lord. Look at how the Lord replied to Joshua in verse 13: "'Get up, sanctify the people, and say, "Sanctify yourselves for tomorrow, because thus says the Lord God of Israel: 'There is an accursed thing in your midst, O Israel; you cannot stand before your enemies until you take away the accursed thing from among you.'"'" Don't miss this: compromise robs us of our moral courage. When we've compromised spiritually, we're not going to have the courage to stand.

Now look at verses 24–25: "Then Joshua, and all Israel with him, took Achan the son of Zerah, the silver, the garment, the wedge of gold, his sons, his daughters, his oxen, his donkeys, his sheep, his tent, and all that he had, and they brought them to the Valley of Achor. And Joshua said, 'Why have you troubled us? The LORD will trouble you this day.' So all Israel stoned him with stones; and they burned them with fire after they had stoned them with stones." There is a debate over this passage as to whether Achan's family was actually stoned with him or just taken to the place of stoning so they could see the consequences of sin. If they were stoned with him, it was probably because they knew of the sin of Achan or they were accomplices to it.

Some would say the punishment of killing him, stoning him, and burning his belongings was harsh. Yes, it was; it was not only to punish him for his sin, but it was to warn others that they needed to obey God in everything. Look at what Joshua said in verse 25: "'Why have you troubled us?'" Now remember, thirty-six innocent men had died as a result of Achan's sin. That's thirty-six families who either lost husbands or fathers. They were dead because one man engaged in what some would describe as a victimless crime. I mean, was it not? He took a garment and some silver and some gold from the owners who were dead. So they weren't offended by what he did. Who could be hurt by a little gold buried in the bottom of their own tent? What harm could that bring? Disobedience to God has consequences for families, for communities, and for nations. There is no such thing as a victimless crime when it is contrary to the instruction of God.

Now after their repentance and dealing with the sin took place, chapter 8 records how Joshua got a word from the Lord, followed the instructions exactly as the Lord commanded, and God gave them victory in the second battle of Ai. It shows that while God's purposes and principles do not change, His tactics and provisions can because in this battle they were permitted to keep the spoil. Joshua was given a different tactic to take the city of Ai, and this time they were successful. But I want us to move on to the end of chapter 8 to point out one more vista.

In the aftermath of their victory over Ai, we find that Joshua took time away from the battlefield to lead Israel into the presence of the Lord to renew the covenant with Him in verses 30–35. Now, this probably seems strange from a strategic perspective. Most modern observers would have counseled the continuation of the military campaign. Capture and control the central section of the land—the hill country. Joshua had his foot on their necks. Why not finish off the enemy now? Yet God's general, sensitive to God's timing, instead led the people on a pilgrimage to meet with the Lord at a predetermined location. In fact, Moses had given specific directions for this before he died (Deut. 27:1–8). As you read what Joshua did with the family of Israel, think of applications to the spiritual leadership of your family: (1) he built an altar; (2) he copied the law of Moses onto several stones; and (3) he read the Word of God to the men and the women, even to the little ones and the foreigners who were with them. Consequently, Joshua set the pace and established the priority of honoring God's Word and offering Him worship.

Leading our families in the daily pursuit of God in the Word and worship is intensely practical. Many Christians often experience defeat in their walk because they fail to prioritize spending time with the Lord, abiding in His Word and praying and worshipping. We must have our spiritual armor on and in place to face the day's battles. Our capacity for overcoming difficulties in life has a direct correlation to our investment in pursuing a relationship with God.

This pursuit was no small thing for Joshua and the people of Israel. After the victory over Ai, the whole nation of men, women, children, and livestock moved from their base camp at Gilgal northward to the Jordan Valley to the place designated by Moses between Mount Ebal (Josh. 8:30) and Mount Gerizim (v. 33), which are at Shechem. This would have been a journey of more than twenty miles. The point is it takes effort; it takes an investment to meet with God. Plus, it was a priority. This spiritual pursuit took precedence over the continuation of the military campaign in which they were engaged. It is the same for us. If we are to succeed in our mission as spiritual leaders, it has to be a priority, and it will necessitate effort and investment.

Why was Shechem chosen as the location? From a practical perspective, this area between the mountains created a natural amphitheater for such a large number of people. This place has outstanding acoustical properties so that people standing on one mountain can be heard by those standing on the other mountain. From a strategic perspective, these mountains are located near the geographic center of the land. Shechem became the central meeting place. More important than its centrality, this location had serious spiritual significance. Abram stopped at the tree of Moreh in Shechem. There, God confirmed His promise to give the land to him, and Abram built an altar at the site (Gen. 12:7). Jacob, Abram's grandson, also built an altar at Shechem, calling it "El Elohe Israel," meaning "mighty God of Israel" (Gen. 33:18–20). And the remains of Jacob's son Joseph were buried at Shechem (Josh. 24:32). So the altar at Shechem was recognized as a "sanctuary of the LORD" (v. 26). Indeed, Shechem was a worship center from this time to when Joshua gave his farewell address (cf. 24:1) and for many years afterward. It is here that Joshua led the people to renew the covenant with God.

That raises a question: Do you have a place and a time that you and your family regularly meet with God? Are you a part of a Bible-centered church? Part of our mission as parents is to lead our families in participation and partnership in a place of worship, a local body of believers. This is what Joshua did with Israel at Shechem. In fact, Moses had already instructed them about what to do back in Deuteronomy 27:11–14. The blessings and the curses from the law were to be read, and the people were to respond with "Amen!" So Mount Ebal stood for cursing, and Mount Gerizim stood for blessing. Consequently, this event between the two mountains formed a huge object lesson. What happened to the Israelites in the land, the future of Israel, was going to depend on where they "lived." Would they live on Mount Ebal, in disobedience and under the curses? Or would they live on Mount Gerizim, in obedience and under God's blessing? As we encourage our family in the Word of God, it is always helpful to remind them that our choices have consequences—blessings if we obey and curses if we disobey.

Here's the key takeaway from Joshua 8:30–35: We must take time daily to shape and mold our families spiritually, and it starts with daily time in the Word and worship. Consider the fact that if you were to worship together as a family at home each day, by the time your child was age eighteen, you would have had more than 6,500 opportunities to read the Scriptures, pray, and sing with him or her. If you read roughly a chapter from the Bible every day for eighteen years, you would read the Bible through at least five and one-half times. Think of the positive cumulative effect on a child or grandchild of simply reading a chapter a day from the Bible. That's why Stand on the Word is such a great pursuit for the whole family.

Questions for Reflection and Discussion

1. Why was Israel defeated when they first went up against Ai?
2. After the victory at Ai, what did Joshua do with the people at Mount Ebal?

Notes on Today's Bible Reading

— Day 9 —

Today's Reading: Joshua 9–10

Verse of the Day

> And there has been no day like that, before it or after it, that the LORD heeded the voice of a man; for the LORD fought for Israel.
>
> *Joshua 10:14*

Please read the entire Scripture selection in your own Bible and highlight or underline verses that stand out to you before you read the observations and engage the questions below.

Today we are in Joshua chapters 9 and 10. These are encouraging passages to me because they show us that even when we don't get it exactly right, the Lord can still use our mistakes to accomplish His purposes if we are following Him. It reminds me of what the apostle Paul wrote over in Romans 8:28: "And we know that all things work together for good to those who love God, to those who are the called according to His purpose."

Let's jump right into this starting in Joshua 9:1–2: "And it came to pass when all the kings who were on this side of the Jordan, in the hills and in the lowland and in all the coasts of the Great Sea toward Lebanon—the Hittite, the Amorite, the Canaanite, the Perizzite, the Hivite, and the Jebusite—heard about it, that they gathered together to fight with Joshua and Israel with one accord." The enemy of God's people found common ground in opposing what God was doing through them, a pattern which continues to this day. And we talked about this before, the tactic that Joshua used going into Jericho by dividing the country. These kingdoms were the city-states in the southern part of Canaan.

Let's pick back up in Joshua 9:3–7:

> But when the inhabitants of Gibeon heard what Joshua had done to Jericho and Ai, they worked craftily, and went and pretended to be ambassadors. And they took old sacks on their donkeys, old wineskins torn and mended, old and patched sandals on their feet, and old garments on themselves; and all the bread of their provision was dry and moldy. And they went to Joshua, to the camp at Gilgal, and said to him and to the men of Israel, "We have come from a far country; now therefore, make a covenant with us." Then the men of Israel said to the Hivites, "Perhaps you dwell among us; so how can we make a covenant with you?"

Remember, they were told not to make covenants in peace with nearby countries in Canaan. If they were far away countries, they could, but not with those countries in the land because God wanted them to remove the idolatry and the wickedness that had polluted the land. But we must give it to the Gibeonites for being creative and also for trusting Israel to be a people of their word if they in fact did enter into a treaty.

Look at Joshua 9:9: "So they said to him: 'From a very far country your servants have come, because of the name of the LORD your God; for we have heard of His fame, and all that He did in Egypt.'"

Word travels fast when the power of God is on the move and they wanted to save their necks. Let's jump to Joshua 9:12–14: "'This bread of ours we took hot for our provision from our houses on the day we departed to come to you. But now look, it is dry and moldy. And these wineskins which we filled were new, and see, they are torn; and these our garments and our sandals have become old because of the very long journey.' Then the men of Israel took some of their provisions; but they did not ask counsel of the LORD."

Here's the error that Israel made—and, quite frankly, we often make. They trusted in what they saw and didn't ask God to reveal to them what was really true. They lacked discernment. They should have had a few of the wives around the discussion table. I have found that my wife can often smell a rat a lot quicker than I can. Bottom line, though, they should have inquired of the Lord before entering into this binding relationship.

So Israel entered into this treaty and then discovered they were actually neighbors. Gibeon was only six and a half miles southwest of Ai. Joshua confronted them for their deception, but he kept his word. He kept the commitment he made to them. As a result, the people of Gibeon were made servants to provide water and wood for the tabernacle, and they were happy to do so because they were able to live. Now this is where it gets exciting. This treaty was the trigger for other kings to act. And they came against Gibeon to punish them for defecting and to draw Israel into a battle. Look at Joshua 10:6–9:

> And the men of Gibeon sent to Joshua at the camp at Gilgal, saying, "Do not forsake your servants; come up to us quickly, save us and help us, for all the kings of the Amorites who dwell in the mountains have gathered together

> against us." So Joshua ascended from Gilgal, he and all the people of war with him, and all the mighty men of valor. And the LORD said to Joshua, "Do not fear them, for I have delivered them into your hand; not a man of them shall stand before you." Joshua therefore came upon them suddenly, having marched all night from Gilgal.

Notice this time Joshua must have inquired of the Lord because the Lord was speaking to him and said, "Do not fear them."

We also see here a tactic Joshua used frequently, and it's been copied. As I have mentioned before, warriors and military leaders throughout history have studied Joshua's tactics. In fact, Stonewall Jackson, who was one of the generals of the South in the Civil War, studied Joshua quite intently and mirrored a lot of his tactics, including this one. Joshua moved his troops over a long distance at night for a surprise attack. He marched his men probably about twenty-five miles that night. The result was a rout the next morning because the Amorites weren't prepared for it. But this is not the end of it.

Let's look at Joshua 10:11–14:

> And it happened, as they fled before Israel and were on the descent of Beth Horon, that the LORD cast down large hailstones from heaven on them as far as Azekah, and they died. There were more who died from the hailstones than the children of Israel killed with the sword. Then Joshua spoke to the LORD in the day when the LORD delivered up the Amorites before the children of Israel, and he said in the sight of Israel:

> "Sun, stand still over Gibeon;
> And Moon, in the Valley of Aijalon."
> So the sun stood still,
> And the moon stopped,
> Till the people had revenge
> Upon their enemies.
>
> Is this not written in the Book of Jasher? So the sun stood still in the midst of heaven, and did not hasten to go down for about a whole day. And there has been no day like that, before it or after it, that the Lord heeded the voice of a man; for the Lord fought for Israel.

In this passage, we find two keys to overcoming the opposition. Number one: Joshua spoke to the Lord. Our prayer life is essential. We have to be in relationship with the Lord through prayer. We cannot neglect our prayer life. Joshua was not going to repeat what he had failed to do in the previous chapter, and that was inquire of the Lord.

The second key to overcoming the opposition was that Joshua stayed in the battle after marching all night and fighting all day. Look at his request: "Let us finish the work. Let the sun stand still." He didn't pray for a break. He didn't pray for relief. He prayed for the opportunity to complete the mission God had given him. Speak to the Lord and stay in the battle.

Now look at the results over in Joshua 10:42: "All these kings and their land Joshua took at one time, because the Lord God of Israel fought for Israel." This is what happens when the Lord fights for you.

Questions for Reflection and Discussion

1. How did the Gibeonites trick Joshua and the leaders into a costly alliance?

2. What did God do to give Joshua time to gain a complete victory over the Amorites?

Notes on Today's Bible Reading

— Day 10 —

Today's Reading: Joshua 11–12

Verse of the Day

> So Joshua took the whole land, according to all that the LORD had said to Moses; and Joshua gave it as an inheritance to Israel according to their divisions by their tribes. Then the land rested from war.
>
> *Joshua 11:23*

Please read the entire Scripture selection in your own Bible and highlight or underline verses that stand out to you before you read the observations and engage the questions below.

Today we are in Joshua 11–12. These are two pretty short chapters. In chapter 11, we have the conquest of the northern city-states. And then in the chapter 12, there's a summary of the victories under Moses on the east side of the Jordan then the victories under Joshua's leadership on the west side of the Jordan, both the southern and northern regions of Canaan.

Let's begin in Joshua 11:1–2: "And it came to pass, when Jabin king of Hazor heard these things, that he sent to Jobab king of Madon, to the king of Shimron, to the king of Achshaph, and to the kings who were from the north, in the mountains, in the plain south of Chinneroth, in the lowland, and in the heights of Dor on the west." So what we see happening here is the same thing that happened in the southern region; a northern coalition formed against Israel as they were moving in and taking over the promised land. Look at Joshua 11:3–6:

> to the Canaanites in the east and in the west, the Amorite, the Hittite, the Perizzite, the Jebusite in the mountains, and the Hivite below Hermon in the land of Mizpah. So they went out, they and all their armies with them, as many people as the sand that is on the seashore in multitude, with very many horses and chariots. And when all these kings had met together, they came and camped together at the waters of Merom to fight against Israel. But the LORD said to Joshua, "Do not be afraid because of them, for tomorrow about this time I will deliver all of them slain before Israel. You shall hamstring their horses and burn their chariots with fire."

Again, King Jabin of Hazor formed a coalition kings and their armies to come against Israel. From a human perspective, the prospects looked grim for Joshua and his forces. This coalition had numerical superiority. According to verse 4, they had a seemingly numberless multitude of warriors. The coalition armies also had tactical superiority. They had horses and chariots.

Yet the Lord spoke to Joshua as he faced what looked like overwhelming odds. He said in verse 6, "Do not be afraid." This is the fourth time God has said that to Joshua (see 1:9; 8:1; 10:8). You know, we read this reassurance from God a lot in Scripture, and we're going to see it many times more. Almost every move of God is preceded by this phrase. Why? Because in those situations where the only hope is for God to move, our faith is challenged. In fact, it's not our default position to go to God. Often times we panic when we look at the overwhelming odds. There's such a thing in psychology as "fight or flight." People will run or they'll immediately fight. Our default position should be to go before the Lord and ask, "Lord, what should we do?" And in this case, He spoke to Joshua and essentially said, "Do not fear. I'm going to take care of this."

Look at verse 7: "So Joshua and all the people of war with him came against them suddenly by the waters of Merom, and they attacked them." Now we don't know all the details of this attack, but we read that Joshua came against them suddenly, as we talked about previously. This was a typical tactic Joshua used, even though it was uncommon at the time. We assume he marched his men through the night a pretty good distance and came upon them when they were unprepared. And again, we see a route like we did last time.

Then we read in verse 8: "And the LORD delivered them into the hand of Israel, who defeated them and chased them to Greater Sidon, to the Brook Misrephoth, and to the Valley of Mizpah eastward; they attacked them until they left none of them remaining." Don't miss this. It says the Lord delivered them into the hand of Israel. You know, the opposition to what God has promised you and me as followers of Jesus Christ is often large. Many are opposed to us, and they are powerful and intimidating. But as we obey and fear God, we need not fear them, for God fights for us. And again, we're talking about in the spiritual. The Lord fights for us and the promises He has for us. We have to pray and pursue those things God has promised you and me in the abundant life that Jesus obtained for us. Joshua provided the model in verse 9a: "So Joshua did to them as the LORD had told him." That is the key.

Notice Joshua "hamstrung their horses and burned their chariots with fire" (v. 9b). To hamstring a horse means to sever a tendon in the leg. It renders the horse unable to charge; it takes some of the strength away. The horse can still be used for farming, but it can no longer be used for fighting. Then we read that Joshua burned the enemy chariots. Now from a purely strategic military perspective, someone might ask, "Why do that? If Israel, didn't have horses and chariots, why hamstring the horses and burn the chariots? Why not use them to defeat the rest of their enemies?" Answer: God wanted them to trust Him rather than horses and chariots. Some five hundred years later, David wrote in Psalm 20:7: "Some trust in chariots, and some in horses; but we will remember the name of the Lord our God."

These next verses and others like them have caused a great deal of consternation:

> Joshua turned back at that time and took Hazor, and struck its king with the sword; for Hazor was formerly the head of all those kingdoms. And they struck all the people who were in it with the edge of the sword, utterly destroying them. There was none left breathing. Then he burned Hazor with fire. So all the cities of those kings, and all their kings, Joshua took and struck with the edge of the sword. He utterly destroyed them, as Moses the servant of the Lord had commanded. (Josh. 11:10–12)

Again, some read this and ask, "Why did God have Joshua kill all these people?" While it is not my purpose to present a full biblical defense of war, I do want to provide a brief, biblical answer. Because of Adam and Eve's sin, we live in a sinful and broken world. By nature, God is holy and must punish sin. Yet God "is longsuffering toward us, not willing that any should perish but that all should come to repentance" (2 Pet. 3:9). Because not all do come to repentance, judgment is necessary. God uses various means to mete out His justice, one of the most extreme of which is war. Sometimes He used His people to punish nations who were evil. Sometimes He used evil nations to punish His own sinful people. What we are reading about in the pages of Joshua is primarily the former case. In fact, God predicted to Abraham all the way back in Genesis 15 that Israel would go into bondage in a foreign land [Egypt] for four hundred years then return to the land of Canaan to reclaim it, even giving the reason behind his timing: "for the iniquity of the Amorites is not yet complete" (v. 16b). During Israel's slavery in Egypt and wanderings in the wilderness, the evil people who inhabited the promised land practiced child sacrifice and gross sexual immorality as a part of their pagan worship. They were given plenty of time and opportunity to repent, but they did not, and all that was left was God's judgment to be meted out through Joshua and his army in warfare.

It's ironic that the same critics who call God unjust for directing Joshua to do this are the same critics who will look around the world and see groups like the Taliban or Hamas committing atrocities and demand, "Well if there's a God, why doesn't He do something about it? Why doesn't He intervene from heaven and punish people like that?" And yet when they read here in Joshua that God did indeed intervene from heaven, they complain, "I can't believe God had Joshua mete out justice to those evil people in such a harsh way." We'll leave it there.

Look at Joshua 11:15 and how Joshua's obedience is characterized: "As the Lord had commanded Moses His servant, so Moses commanded Joshua, and so Joshua did. He left nothing undone of all that the LORD had commanded Moses." Joshua followed God's commands completely, without compromising or neglecting anything. We can learn from Joshua's example to do the same. Then verse 16a gives us the result: "Thus Joshua took all this land." He enjoyed God's favor in battle after battle because he faithfully carried out God's directives. If we obey God, we will experience God's favor as well. Just don't let anyone tell you the battles will always be quick and easy. We read in verse 18, "Joshua made war a long time with all those kings." Finally, verse 23 provides a fitting summary: "So Joshua took the whole land, according to all that the LORD had said to Moses; and Joshua gave it as an inheritance to Israel according to their divisions by their tribes. Then the land rested from war."

Chapter 12 gives us a detailed accounting of kings and kingdoms who were defeated by Moses and Joshua tagged to the geography of the land on the east and west sides of the Jordan, respectively. Up until now, we have only seen the "highlight reel" of major battles. Here we are given a complete record of the rulers, nations, and the geography that was conquered by the armies of Israel empowered by the Lord. In addition to the two kings defeated under Moses, God enabled Joshua and the Israelites to conquer thirty-one kings and their cities and to possess the land that He had sworn to their fathers. We can learn from this example to recall and rejoice in the ways that God has delivered us from our enemies and given us His blessings.

Questions for Reflection and Discussion

1. What did the Lord tell Joshua when all the kings and their armies met at the waters of Merom to fight against Israel?
2. Why did Joshua and the Israelites not battle some of the Hivites?

Notes on Today's Bible Reading

— Day 11 —

Today's Reading: Joshua 13–15

Verse of the Day

> "Now therefore, give me this mountain of which the LORD spoke in that day; for you heard in that day how the Anakim were there, and that the cities were great and fortified. It may be that the LORD will be with me, and I shall be able to drive them out as the LORD said."
>
> *Joshua 14:12*

Please read the entire Scripture selection in your own Bible and highlight or underline verses that stand out to you before you read the observations and engage the questions below.

Today we are in Joshua 13–15. In the latter portion of chapter 13, we have the division of the land for the Reubenites, the Gaddites, and half the tribe of Manasseh on the east side of the Jordan River. Then in chapters 14 and 15, we see the beginning of the division of Canaan, starting with the tribe of Judah.

Let's begin in Joshua 13:1: "Now Joshua was old, advanced in years. And the LORD said to him: 'You are old, advanced in years, and there remains very much land yet to be possessed.'" Now when God tells you that you're old, you must be old. Exactly how old was Joshua? At this point, we're not certain, but it's safe to estimate he was somewhere between the age of 90 and 100. I am not convinced this is speaking to his physical or mental ability. As we will see in a moment, Caleb was the same age as Joshua, and he was still raring to go.

More than anything, I believe God was telling Joshua, "You're old, and there's still much work to be done. Your time is short. Get busy." Now don't miss this. This may be for you. We all need to be reminded of the shortness of life so that we will stay focused on the mission God has given us and the priorities associated with that mission, which He has set out for us. Moses prayed this, and it's recorded in Psalm 90:12: "So teach us to number our days, that we may gain a heart of wisdom." Moses lived to be 120 years old, and he was saying, "Lord, help me to count my days, so I will be focused on what you've given me to do."

A couple of realities are here that may seem in conflict, but they're not. As we will see, the children of Israel did not possess all God had given them. In fact, they only occupied a small portion, about 10 percent, of the land God promised to them, even at the zenith of the kingdom under David and Solomon. However, occupying all the land was to be their priority. There were clearly setbacks, both external and internal. Giants and enemies were in the land and had to be overcome, and there was the ever-present threat of spiritual compromise, which, as we know, led to their ultimate downfall.

Now keeping in mind that the Old Testament speaks to the physical, where the New Testament speaks to the spiritual, the promised land for us is not a picture of heaven but the abundant life we have here and now through Jesus Christ. But we have to go in and possess it. Paul talks about this in Ephesians 1:3: "Blessed be the God and Father of our Lord Jesus Christ, who has blessed us with every spiritual blessing in the heavenly places in Christ." But will we fully experience those blessings in this life? Will our work ever be done? Look what Paul said in Philippians 3:12–14: "Not that I have already attained, or am already perfected; but I press on, that I may lay hold of that for which Christ Jesus has also laid hold of me. Brethren, I do not count myself to have apprehended; but one thing I do, forgetting those things which are behind and reaching forward to those things which are ahead, I press toward the goal for the prize of the upward call of God in Christ Jesus."

I doubt we'll ever come to a place where we can say, "Oh, I have accomplished everything. God's work is finished." There certainly comes a time when our part in the work is done and then the Lord takes us home. But we need to be mindful of the shortness of our time. We don't need to waste our time. I'm not saying we don't need to relax and refresh, but you know what? A lot of Christians spend way too much time watching television or are engaged in sports and other mindless activities. I know I may be offending some with this, but God has not called us to be spectators. He has called us to be participants in the great unfolding of His work on this earth. Time is short. There is a lot to be done. The fields are ripe unto the harvest, as Jesus said.

Now let's move on to Joshua 14 and Joshua's colleague Caleb.

> Then the children of Judah came to Joshua in Gilgal. And Caleb the son of Jephunneh the Kenizzite said to him: "You know the word which the Lord said to Moses the man of God concerning you and me in Kadesh Barnea. I was forty years old when Moses the servant of the Lord sent me from Kadesh Barnea to spy out the land, and I brought back word to him as it was in my heart. Nevertheless my brethren who went up with me made the heart of the people

> melt, but I wholly followed the LORD my God. So Moses swore on that day, saying, 'Surely the land where your foot has trodden shall be your inheritance and your children's forever, because you have wholly followed the LORD my God.' And now, behold, the LORD has kept me alive, as He said, these forty-five years, ever since the LORD spoke this word to Moses while Israel wandered in the wilderness; and now, here I am this day, eighty-five years old. As yet I am as strong this day as on the day that Moses sent me; just as my strength was then, so now is my strength for war, both for going out and for coming in. Now therefore, give me this mountain of which the LORD spoke in that day; for you heard in that day how the Anakim were there, and that the cities were great and fortified. It may be that the LORD will be with me, and I shall be able to drive them out as the LORD said." (vv. 6–11)

As we read, he takes the land. So what can we take away from this? Caleb, like Joshua, wholly followed the Lord. And look who was left of their generation, just the two of them. They were the only two. Their class reunion was pretty small. They were faithful to God, and God was faithful to them. I hear all the time, "Tony, aren't you afraid you're on the wrong side of history with all this stuff regarding marriage and human sexuality?" No, I'm not. I am on the side of the Author of history, the One who writes history. And I'm not afraid to stand alone. And you shouldn't be afraid to stand alone either as long as you're standing on the truth of God's Word. Joshua and Caleb took on one of their most significant assignments around the age most people are when looking for cemetery plots. I mean, Caleb was eighty-five years old, and he said, "Give me that mountain."

Here's how I see Caleb based upon this passage. With anticipation, he lived waiting for the fulfillment of God's promise. That anticipation had him in preparation. He said, "I am as strong as I was the day Moses sent me to spy out the land." And I think he wasn't just talking about physical strength but also about mental and spiritual strength. I think he was strong. He was in tip-top shape. We need to be in shape, so we can accomplish what God has for us. And oftentimes it doesn't come until near the end of our lives. We see this repeatedly through Scripture.

I remember a number of years ago when I was only a couple of years out of high school, and it was before my three-year enlistment in the Marine Corps. I was in a 10k, and I was huffing and puffing along. All of a sudden a man passed me, and he was about eighty years old, zipping by me. It was a pivotal moment for me. After this, I realized I needed to make some changes. That was almost forty years ago, and today I live anticipating seeing God's promises by preparing physically and spiritually. Every day I spend my first three hours or more in prayer, Bible study, and physical fitness. I share this only to encourage you to be prepared to seize the moment when God wants to fulfill those promises in your life. We need to live with anticipation of God accomplishing what He has promised.

Questions for Reflection and Discussion

1. What was the basis for Moses' promise to Caleb that the land he had walked on would be his and his children's inheritance?

2. What was Caleb relying upon to drive the Anakim [giants] out of the land?

Notes on Today's Bible Reading

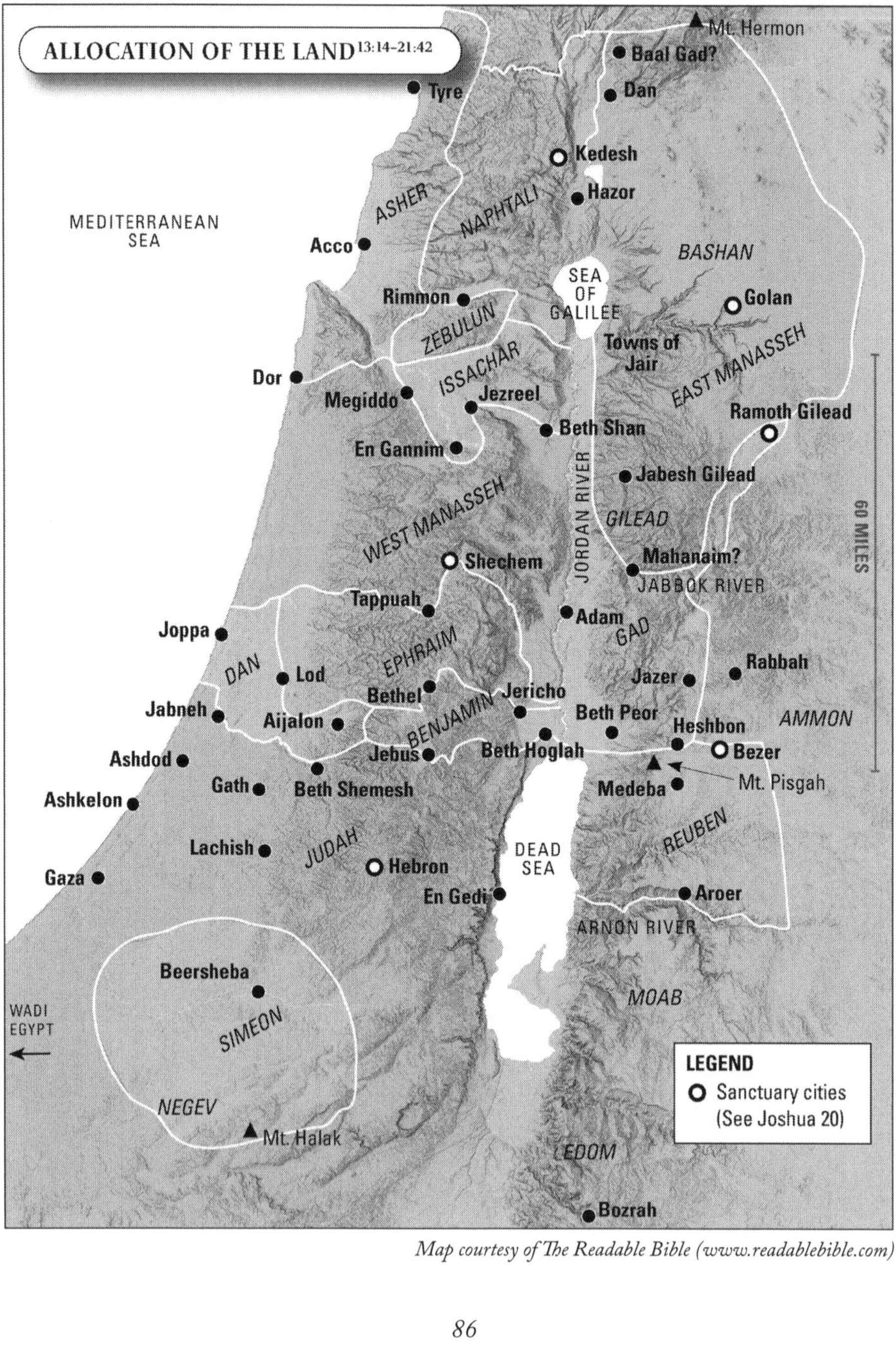

Map courtesy of The Readable Bible (www.readablebible.com)

— Day 12 —

Today's Reading: Joshua 16–19

Verse of the Day

> These were the inheritances which Eleazar the priest, Joshua the son of Nun, and the heads of the fathers of the tribes of the children of Israel divided as an inheritance by lot in Shiloh before the LORD, at the door of the tabernacle of meeting. So they made an end of dividing the country.
>
> *Joshua 19:51*

Please read the entire Scripture selection in your own Bible and highlight or underline verses that stand out to you before you read the observations and engage the questions below.

Today we are in Joshua 16–19, which are relatively short chapters. We're moving into the heart of the land allotment to the various tribes. Today we have the tribe of Ephraim, the half tribe of Manasseh, and the tribe of Benjamin. Now keep in mind what we've discussed before. The promised land does not represent heaven for the New Testament believer. I know this is sometimes the common thought. We hear the songs of standing on Jordan's stormy banks and crossing over as if that were into heaven. This is not the case. What the promised land represents to the New Testament believer is the abundant life that Jesus Christ, Yeshua (the same as Joshua in the Old Testament, meaning "Yahweh is salvation"), came to bring us. We are saved by grace alone through faith. That's it; we're saved by grace. Israel didn't earn the land; it was given to them. But the possession of it required their pursuit of God. And so it is with us. If we want to possess all God has for us, we must walk in His ways and take hold of all He has intended for us to have.

Now let's look at the last verse of chapter 16. Joshua 16:10 says, "And they did not drive out the Canaanites who dwelt in Gezer; but the Canaanites dwell among the Ephraimites to this day and have become forced laborers." This is loaded with meaning. They did not drive them out. Please mark this because we're going to come back to it in subsequent books. We have not by any means heard the last of this matter. God was quite specific in telling them to remove the inhabitants of the land. Remember, they were to remove the inhabitants lest they become influenced by them and drawn away from God.

Next look at Joshua 17:12–13: "Yet the children of Manasseh could not drive out the inhabitants of those cities, but the Canaanites were determined to dwell in that land. And it happened, when the children of Israel grew strong, that they put the Canaanites to forced labor, but did not utterly drive them out." See, Manasseh failed to do the same thing, and in that they planted the seeds of their own destruction. But look at what they did next: "Then the children of Joseph spoke to Joshua, saying, 'Why have you given us only one lot and one share to inherit, since we are a great people, inasmuch as the Lord has blessed us until now?'" (v. 14). Wait a minute. They were given land, but they didn't possess it. Why? Well, it was too difficult, so they simply asked for more land. Why not ask for help in taking possession of the land they had already been given?

Before we become too critical of the Israelites, however, let's do some self-evaluation. Have you ever heard someone say, "I'm looking for God's direction for my life"? Or maybe you've said this. The first question I believe in helping them find that direction is this: "Are you in the Word of God?" See, the Word of God is just that. It is God's Word. It provides direction for our lives. It gives us guidance on how we should live, how we should raise our children, how we should do our work, how we should spend our time. And here's the reality: God is not going to give us more direction until we have used what He's given us. We have in our hands the means to live in the abundant life that Jesus has provided, and it is obedience to God's Word.

Let's continue in Joshua 17:15–18:

> So Joshua answered them, "If you are a great people, then go up to the forest country and clear a place for yourself there in the land of the Perizzites and the giants, since the mountains of Ephraim are too confined for you." But the children of Joseph said, "The mountain country is not enough for us; and all the Canaanites who dwell in the land of the valley have chariots of iron, both those who are of Beth Shean and its towns and those who are of the Valley of Jezreel." And Joshua spoke to the house of Joseph—to Ephraim and Manasseh—saying, "You are a great people and have great power; you shall not have only one lot, but the mountain country shall be yours. Although it is wooded, you shall cut it down, and its farthest extent shall be yours; for you shall drive out the Canaanites, though they have iron chariots and are strong."

A little sarcasm may be in Joshua's response. I can't prove that, but it seems so. Yes, you can have more land. You can have the mountains with the giants. I don't think this is what they wanted to hear. I do think in his response, though, he was affirming them or at least challenging them to be all they could be. You are a great people, and you have great power, but you have to act upon it. Yes, you're blessed; you've got a double portion. You were blessed, but you have to act upon it.

This is similar to us in the New Testament as believers. Paul wrote this to the Corinthians in 2 Corinthians 10:4–5: "For the weapons of our warfare *are* not carnal but mighty in God for pulling down strongholds, casting down arguments and every high thing that exalts itself against the knowledge of God, bringing every thought into captivity to the obedience of Christ." You see, the weapons we have been given to take the land, spiritually speaking, are powerful. Now, what does this mean? It means we have what we need to take the land, our heritage, our families, our children, our communities. But it's not going to be handed to us. These things, we can pray about and we should. But we must act as well. We have to act in faith to obtain what the Lord has given us. And I believe in this abundant life we're not to live as meager believers, just barely getting by. I'm not talking about material blessings. Material blessings are passing—here today and gone tomorrow. I'm talking about the significance of life, abundant life, meaning our lives have purpose. Our lives have meaning that every day we get up with a sense of who we are, our identity, and we are indeed blessed by God with a sense of who we are, a sense of what we've been called to and where we are going.

Many people today aimlessly wander through this world. That's why drug addiction is at an all-time high. That's why sexually transmitted diseases are at record levels. People are looking for fulfillment. They're looking for the abundant life that is evasive of those who are outside of Christ. And quite frankly, many in Christ don't find it because they're not willing to possess it, because it requires that we walk in obedience to God and do what He has told us to do. This may sound legalistic, but it's not. We're not trying to earn our salvation. But Jesus said, "If you love Me, you'll keep My commandments." Powerful word, powerful illustration—a parallel to how we as believers in the New Testament should be living.

Joshua 19 concludes the allotment of the land in Canaan to the tribes. Here we have the tribes of Simeon, Zebulun, Issachar, Asher, Napthali, and Dan. And this chapter includes various lists of cities and villages included in the inheritance to the different tribes. So I will be brief with a couple of observations. First, a general observation from all the folks whom we've seen being placed on the boundaries of these internal tribes or what we could call states. We're led to understand that borders matter. Without borders, we don't have a country; we don't have a state. Borders and boundaries are associated with identity. Those who want to do away with boundaries and borders suggest more of a globalist approach to the world, and they're attempting to supplant our identity. Now, don't be led to believe the amalgamation of countries is somehow a Christian idea or a biblical concept, or that it's compassionate. The gospel is for all people in all places, but the decentralization of mankind is actually a biblical concept. We see this because it is a check on evil. Just think, if we were all citizens of Russia, who would keep Russia in check? This was what happened at the tower of Babel. So we see this as the focus going into the promised land, the borders that were established for the promised land for all of Israel. And then it was divided up with boundaries for each of the tribes.

Many names are in this chapter, but I encourage you to read the whole chapter because some things are tucked in every now and then between the list of names. I want to focus on one verse in particular because this is one of those things that has a little history to it. Look at Joshua 19:9: "The inheritance of the children of Simeon was included in the share of the children of Judah, for the share of the children of Judah was too much for them. Therefore the children of Simeon had their inheritance within the inheritance of that people." I point this out because whether the allocation was made because it was realized that Judah had too much to manage, they couldn't handle it, or it was for some other reason, this was the fulfillment of Jacob's prophecy in Genesis 49. Look at verse 5:

> "Simeon and Levi are brothers;
> Instruments of cruelty are in their dwelling place."

That's a reference to what they did in Genesis 34 in Shechem, where they actually massacred all the men of the city. Now look at Genesis 49:6–7:

> "Let not my soul enter their council;
> Let not my honor be united to their assembly;
> For in their anger they slew a man,
> And in their self-will they hamstrung an ox.
> Cursed be their anger, for it is fierce;
> And their wrath, for it is cruel!
> I will divide them in Jacob
> And scatter them in Israel."

This is exactly what happened in their allotment in the promised land in Joshua 19. And it's another reminder that God's Word, in this case given through Jacob, does not return void. God's Word will be accomplished.

Questions for Reflection and Discussion

1. Because the tribe of Manasseh was unable to drive out all the Canaanites, what did the tribe ultimately do with them?
2. At this point, how many tribes had not yet taken possession of the land given to them, and what was Joshua's solution?

Notes on Today's Bible Reading

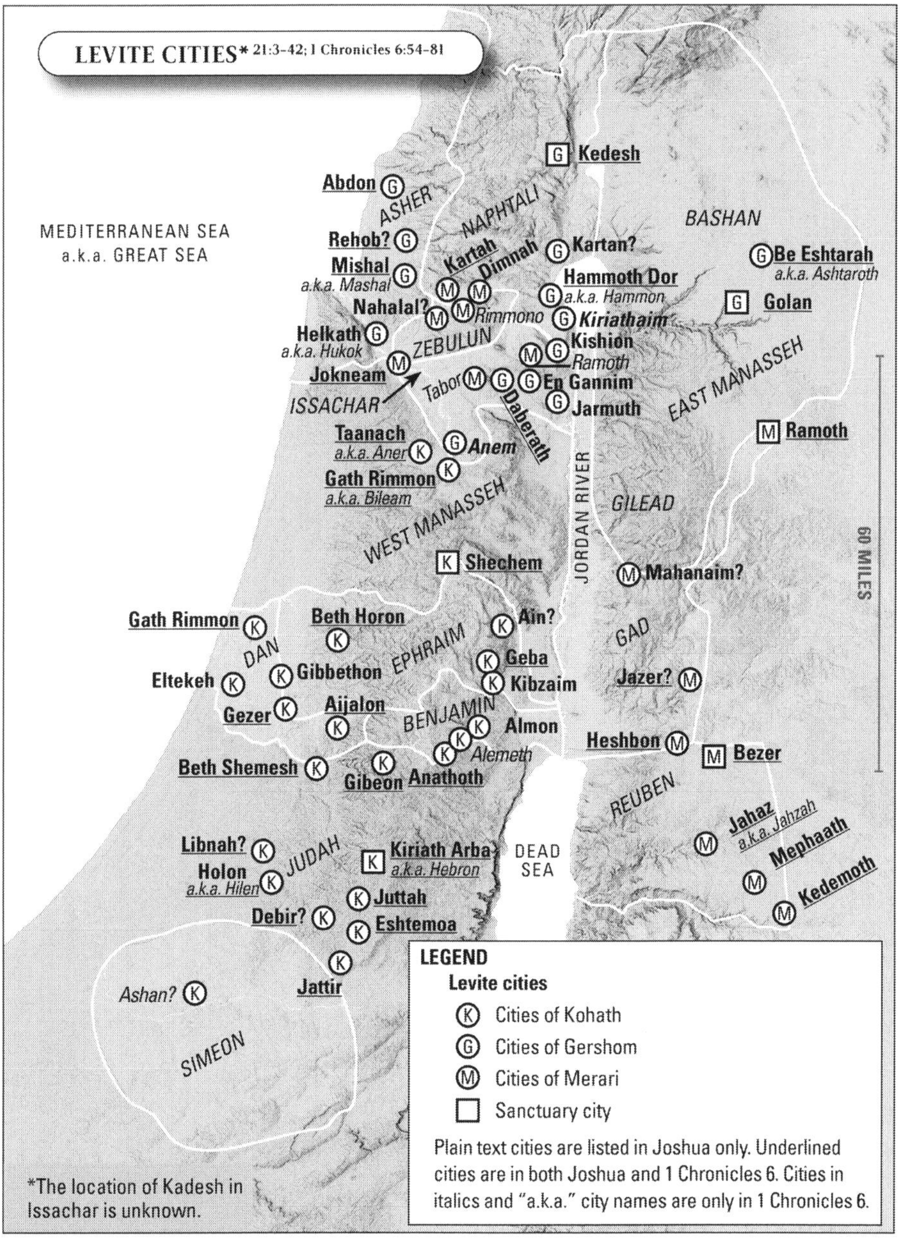

Map courtesy of The Readable Bible (www.readablebible.com)

— Day 13 —

Today's Reading: Joshua 20–21

Verse of the Day

> Not a word failed of any good thing which the LORD had spoken to the house of Israel. All came to pass.
>
> *Joshua 21:45*

Please read the entire Scripture selection in your own Bible and highlight or underline verses that stand out to you before you read the observations and engage the questions below.

Today we are in Joshua 20 and 21. In chapter 20, Joshua and the Israelites were instructed to establish the cities of refuge. This was something we also read in Numbers 35, which God first told Moses about. And so now they had conquered the land, and they had allocated the land. Establishing cities of refuge is one of the first things they were set to do. In Joshua 21, we have the allotment of forty-eight cities to the Levites (v. 41), who were not given a regular allotment like the other tribes. Remember, their inheritance was not so much the land as it was the Lord (see Deut. 18:2).

Let's begin in Joshua 20:1–6:

> The LORD also spoke to Joshua, saying, "Speak to the children of Israel, saying: 'Appoint for yourselves cities of refuge,

> of which I spoke to you through Moses, that the slayer who kills a person accidentally or unintentionally may flee there; and they shall be your refuge from the avenger of blood. And when he flees to one of those cities, and stands at the entrance of the gate of the city, and declares his case in the hearing of the elders of that city, they shall take him into the city as one of them, and give him a place, that he may dwell among them. Then if the avenger of blood pursues him, they shall not deliver the slayer into his hand, because he struck his neighbor unintentionally, but did not hate him beforehand. And he shall dwell in that city until he stands before the congregation for judgment, and until the death of the one who is high priest in those days. Then the slayer may return and come to his own city and his own house, to the city from which he fled.'"

We focused on the purposes of the cities when we were in the book of Numbers, but I want to touch on this again because the practical purpose of these cities was simply to establish justice.

These were not the sanctuary cities we see popping up across America today, which provide those who are breaking the law with safe haven, enabling them to evade justice. On the contrary, cities of refuge were established to ensure justice by protecting the innocent and punishing those who spilled innocent blood and keeping the land from being polluted with the spilling of innocent blood. We've talked before about the avenger of blood, who was a near relative obligated to basically kill someone who had killed a family member. The six cities of refuge—three on the east side and three on the west side—allowed someone who killed an individual to run to the nearest city of refuge and find shelter until the congregation of the city where the event occurred could hear the facts in the case and then render a decision (see Josh. 20:7–9). If it was determined to be premeditated murder, his life was not to be spared. He was to be executed. If the death he caused was accidental, he then returned to a city of refuge, and as long as he stayed in that city, he was protected. He could only leave free from the threat of an avenger of blood after the death of the high priest. So this is the practical purpose. But there's a spiritual application here. Remember, the Old Testament speaks to the physical, whereas the New Testament speaks to the spiritual. So we gain spiritual principles from this. This is a tremendous picture and illustration of Jesus Christ. He is our refuge. He is our city of refuge, where we run and find safety. And as the death of the earthly high priest freed the slayer from being confined to the city of refuge and from the avenger of blood, so the death of our High Priest, Jesus Christ, frees us from the penalty of sin and death. This is a tremendous illustration of what we have in Jesus Christ.

Chapter 21 is another account of what God had previously told them to do once they came into the land of promise. We've seen most of this before, but now that they had the land and it had been allocated, Joshua was following up saying, "All right, this is what we're to do next. Remember what Moses said?" So here we have the allotment of forty-eight cities to the Levites who were not given a regular allotment like the other tribes. Theirs was to be taken from the other tribe so that they were intermingled and dispersed throughout the entire country, really as salt and light to be constantly reminding people of their spiritual obligation and spiritual heritage. This was a part of their role.

As we finish up, let's look at Joshua 21:43–45: "So the LORD gave to Israel all the land of which He had sworn to give to their fathers, and they took possession of it and dwelt in it. The LORD gave them rest all around, according to all that He had sworn to their fathers. And not a man of all their enemies stood against them; the LORD delivered all their enemies into their hand. Not a word failed of any good thing which the Lord had spoken to the house of Israel. All came to pass." God did exactly what He said He would do. Here's what we can take away from this: We can count on the Word of God. It will never fail.

Now the history of Israel would have been much different had they continued in this vein of obedience and in faith from generation to generation. They would have had a story to tell of God's goodness and blessing and prosperity in the land. And the same is true for us. If we want to go from generation to generation enjoying the abundant life, the blessings God has given, it requires faith and obedience being passed from one generation to the next. And we're going to see this theme a lot as we go through the Old Testament, the books of Judges and Kings, and as we look at Samuel and the life of the nation of Israel. This is an amazing story, but always be looking at it from a standpoint of the spiritual principles that have application to us. Also remember this: God's Word never fails. What He says, He will do.

Questions for Reflection and Discussion

1. What was the purpose of the cities of refuge?

2. How many cities were given to the Levites?

Notes on Today's Bible Reading

— Day 14 —

Today's Reading: Joshua 22–23

Verse of the Day

> The children of Reuben and the children of Gad called the altar, Witness, "For it is a witness between us that the Lord is God."
>
> *Joshua 22:34*

Please read the entire Scripture selection in your own Bible and highlight or underline verses that stand out to you before you read the observations and engage the questions below.

Today we are in Joshua 22–23. In chapter 22, the tribes from the east side of the Jordan—the Reubenites, the Gadites, and the half tribe of Manasseh—were dismissed from their military obligation as the land on the west side of the Jordan had been conquered. There is not complete certainty, but best estimates are that they spent somewhere between six and seven years in the conquest of the land. Then in chapter 23, Joshua gathered the leaders of the twelve tribes to begin his farewell address.

Let's begin with Joshua 22:1–6:

> Then Joshua called the Reubenites, the Gadites, and half the tribe of Manasseh, and said to them: "You have kept

> all that Moses the servant of the LORD commanded you, and have obeyed my voice in all that I commanded you. You have not left your brethren these many days, up to this day, but have kept the charge of the commandment of the LORD your God. And now the LORD your God has given rest to your brethren, as He promised them; now therefore, return and go to your tents and to the land of your possession, which Moses the servant of the LORD gave you on the other side of the Jordan. But take careful heed to do the commandment and the law which Moses the servant of the LORD commanded you, to love the LORD your God, to walk in all His ways, to keep His commandments, to hold fast to Him, and to serve Him with all your heart and with all your soul." So Joshua blessed them and sent them away, and they went to their tents.

Recall when they asked for their possession on the east side of the Jordan, they said, "Wait a minute. Are you trying to back out of the obligation to go into the promised land?" And they said, "No, no, no, we'll go." So for the past six to seven years, they had been fighting for their families and their crops and their herds on the other side of the Jordan. Now they had completed their mission. But don't miss Joshua's parting advice to these battle-hardened warriors. What did he tell them? He said in Joshua 22:5, "'[T]ake careful heed to do the commandment and the law which Moses the servant of the LORD commanded you, to love the LORD your God, to walk in all His ways, to keep His commandments, to hold fast to Him, and to serve Him with all your heart and with all your soul.'" Of all of the things Joshua could focus on in his final words to his men, this was it: keep the Lord first. There is no question Joshua was consistent in this message from start to finish. We must be intentional about our walk with the Lord, and as leaders we should challenge others to do the same. Pastors should be challenging their congregations. Sunday school teachers should be challenging their class members. Parents should be challenging their children. Dads should be challenging their families. We need to be challenged to keep the Lord first. Joshua knew if they focused on the fundamentals, everything else would fall into place.

Now we have quite an interesting incident in the remainder of this chapter, as the two and a half tribes set up an altar of remembrance on the border—a reminder to future generations of their connection to those who were on the west side of the Jordan. Look at Joshua 22:10–12:

> And when they came to the region of the Jordan which is in the land of Canaan, the children of Reuben, the children of Gad, and half the tribe of Manasseh built an altar there by the Jordan—a great, impressive altar. Now the children of Israel heard someone say, "Behold, the children of Reuben, the children of Gad, and half the tribe of Manasseh have built an altar on the frontier of the land of Canaan, in the region of the Jordan—on the children of Israel's side." And when the children of Israel heard of it, the whole congregation of the children of Israel gathered together at Shiloh to go to war against them.

When word spread of the altar they had built, the remaining tribes gathered at Shiloh, which was where the tabernacle had been erected, and as such it was really the center of national life. Because they saw this as rebellion against God, they were ready to go to war with the very men they had been fighting alongside. Sacrifices on another altar were a direct violation of God's instructions and the first step into apostasy and idolatry. Their reaction, quite frankly, is encouraging. Too bad they lost the zeal they showed here in this situation for the Lord. And as time went on, however, in this case it was a false alarm. The men of Reuben, Gad, and Manasseh would have been wise to alert the other tribes of their intention. But, you know, I'd venture to say maybe they were thinking this would be a pleasant surprise for them. It wasn't.

The tribes on the west side sent a delegation led by Phineas to inquire about the intentions of the two and a half tribes, and look at what Phineas and the tribal leaders had to say in Joshua 22:17–18: "'Is the iniquity of Peor not enough for us, from which we are not cleansed till this day, although there was a plague in the congregation of the LORD, but that you must turn away this day from following the LORD? And it shall be, if you rebel today against the LORD, that tomorrow He will be angry with the whole congregation of Israel.'" This is making reference to the incident with Balaam and Balak regarding power (see Numbers 22–24). And this incident actually appears several times in both the Old Testament and the New Testament. Recall, this was where the men engaged in the idolatry and its related sexual immorality with the temple prostitutes, the result being twenty-four thousand people dying. And in a short period of time, Phineas stood up and intervened, and the plague was stopped. This incident of their sin and God's wrath left an indelible mark upon them. And at this point, it was still fresh enough to motivate them to action.

There's a lesson here about resolving perceived wrongs. The tribes on the west side, although worked up and ready for battle, first inquired and got the facts, which brought about a resolution we read in Joshua 22:33–34: "So the thing pleased the children of Israel, and the children of Israel blessed God; they spoke no more of going against them in battle, to destroy the land where the children of Reuben and Gad dwelt. The children of Reuben and the children of Gad called the altar, Witness, 'For it is a witness between us that the LORD is God.'" We need to be careful how we react to information we receive about what other believers are doing or not doing. Frankly, a lot of information on the internet today is simply not true. It may have an element of truth, but like verse 11 reads in this chapter: "Now the children of Israel heard someone say, 'Behold, the children of Reuben, the children of Gad, and half the tribe of Manasseh have built an altar on the frontier of the land of Canaan.'" Yes, they had built an altar but not for the purposes they were led to believe. Be zealous for God and His Word, but be discerning and wise.

In chapter 23, Joshua gives his farewell address to the leadership of the confederation—all the leaders of the twelve tribes. Like Moses, Joshua recounted their history. I think this is important. We need to go back over our history and show what God has done. God has done many things in this nation of ours. Our children need to know about it. This is why what's being taught in our classrooms is so important. So Joshua went over the history, God's faithfulness to them, and then he challenged them to obey God. In verse 6, we see Joshua charging the leaders with what he had been charged with about thirty years previously: "Therefore be very courageous to keep and to do all that is written in the Book of the Law of Moses, lest you turn aside from it to the right hand or to the left." Courage was needed to obey God when they crossed over into the promised land. And courage to obey God was needed if they were to stay in the promised land and prosper. They needed courage to obey God then, and we need courage to obey God now.

Questions for Reflection and Discussion

1. Why did the Israelites on the west side of the Jordan become upset when they heard the tribes of Reuben, Gad, and Manasseh built an altar on the other side of the Jordan?

2. As a part of his final address to the leaders, Joshua told them to be very courageous and do what?

Notes on Today's Bible Reading

— Day 15 —

Today's Reading: Joshua 24

Verse of the Day

> "And if it seems evil to you to serve the LORD, choose for yourselves this day whom you will serve, whether the gods which your fathers served that were on the other side of the River, or the gods of the Amorites, in whose land you dwell. But as for me and my house, we will serve the LORD."
>
> *Joshua 24:15*

Please read the entire Scripture selection in your own Bible and highlight or underline verses that stand out to you before you read the observations and engage the questions below.

Today we finish up the book of Joshua with chapter 24. The book ends the way it began, and that is with a charge. And I admire Joshua because he started strong and he finished strong. Too many men, too many believers, start out strong, but they finish with a whimper if they finish at all. I believe we should be like the apostle Paul who basically said, "Look, I'm going to cross the finish line with all I have." You know, we need to run this race, this race we call life, with everything we have. We need to run to win. As Paul said, Joshua ran to win. He did not compromise on God's Word.

He didn't cower in the face of opposition. Quite frankly, he didn't care what others thought about his obedience to God. He didn't care who stood with him. He was committed to serving the Lord.

Joshua starts in chapter 24 with a brief overview of their history once again and what God had done for them, including giving them the promised land. Again, I think we should be telling our children the stories of God's faithfulness to us personally and as a nation as well. Look at Joshua 24:13: "'I have given you a land for which you did not labor, and cities which you did not build, and you dwell in them; you eat of the vineyards and olive groves which you did not plant.'" And we've read about this, the more than one hundred cities that they came in and just took possession of and everything that was already done for them. God gave it to them as He drove the inhabitants out of the land previous to them because of their sin and their iniquity. God's grace made entering the promised land possible. He gave it to them. They didn't earn it. They didn't do anything to deserve it. He gave it to them, which is the same for us entering into salvation. But to enjoy the promised land and to dwell in it, obedience to God is required. That's what was required in order to enjoy the blessings God had.

Let's look at Joshua 24:14–15:

> "Now therefore, fear the LORD, serve Him in sincerity and in truth, and put away the gods which your fathers served on the other side of the River and in Egypt. Serve the LORD! And if it seems evil to you to serve the LORD, choose for yourselves this day whom you will serve, whether the gods which your fathers served that were on the other side of the River, or the gods of the Amorites, in whose land you dwell. But as for me and my house, we will serve the LORD."

I love this passage. This is what I was saying about finishing strong. Joshua was about to die at the age of 110 years old, and he was still leading by example. He said, "You can choose who you're going to serve. But as for me and my house, we will serve the Lord."

Look at Joshua 24:16–17: "So the people answered and said: 'Far be it from us that we should forsake the LORD to serve other gods; for the LORD our God is He who brought us and our fathers up out of the land of Egypt, from the house of bondage, who did those great signs in our sight, and preserved us in all the way that we went and among all the people through whom we passed.'" Then drop down to Joshua 24:23, "'Now therefore,' he said, 'put away the foreign gods which are among you, and incline your heart to the LORD God of Israel.'" This suggests that some of the people had already drifted toward idolatry. You know, it does not take long. And we're beginning to see a cycle we will see prominently in the next book, the book of Judges. Peace and prosperity, unfortunately, lead to spiritual complacency, which then leads to moral corruption, which leads to political disorder and chaos. And we're seeing this, quite frankly, in America today. The principles we see in Scripture here and the effects of neglecting those principles are universal. And we're seeing them in America today.

Let's continue in Joshua 24:24–27:

> And the people said to Joshua, "The LORD our God we will serve, and His voice we will obey!" So Joshua made a covenant with the people that day, and made for them a statute and an ordinance in Shechem. Then Joshua wrote these words in the Book of the Law of God. And he took a large stone, and set it up there under the oak that was by the sanctuary of the LORD. And Joshua said to all the people,

> "Behold, this stone shall be a witness to us, for it has heard all the words of the LORD which He spoke to us. It shall therefore be a witness to you, lest you deny your God."

Notice how these monuments and stones were used as reminders of past events and commitments. He led them through a renewal of a covenant—a kind of revival of their obligation and their commitment to the Lord. And he set up this stone as a reminder. This is why the destruction and the removal of monuments in our country today is yet another warning sign of a society forgetting its past so that it can be free to do whatever it pleases or whatever it thinks. I mean, there's a consequence to this. Of course, we'll see this unfold in the life of the nation of Israel.

Then we come to verse 29: "Now it came to pass after these things that Joshua the son of Nun, the servant of the LORD, died, being one hundred and ten years old." Then look at verse 31: "Israel served the LORD all the days of Joshua, and all the days of the elders who outlived Joshua, who had known all the works of the LORD which He had done for Israel." Now this is quite a telling verse. They walked faithfully as long as Joshua was alive, and those who had served with Joshua and had seen the power of God. After that, the drift began. To walk faithfully with God, each generation must experience the power of God. The faith of our fathers gives context, but it is our personal faith in the Lord Jesus Christ that will keep the next generation serving the Lord. This is why Moses and Joshua and others sounded like broken records in charging parents to teach and to lead their children in knowing and walking with the Lord.

America's only hope is the Lord Jesus Christ. It's the gospel. It's the truth of God's Word. And the only way that's going to be disseminated is in the home through parents. And pastors need to be challenging parents to do what God has given them the responsibility and the authority to do, and that is to train up their children. Again, may we live up to the challenge of Joshua: "As for me and my house, we will serve the Lord." And like Joshua, may we finish strong!

Questions for Reflection and Discussion

1. In his final words to the people, Joshua told them to:
    a. Fear the Lord
    b. Serve the Lord
    c. Reject idolatry
    d. All of the above

2. What declaration did Joshua make that displayed his godly leadership in his home?

Notes on Today's Bible Reading

Appendix 1:
Stand on the Word Bible Reading Plan

Visit frc.org/Bible for our chronological journey through the Bible that we call "Stand on the Word." We encourage you to spend time reading and studying the Bible because it is literally "God-breathed" (2 Tim. 3:16); it is God's very words to us. The Bible answers the big questions, such as, Why am I here? Where did I come from? Where am I going (life after death)? If God is good, why does evil and suffering exist? The Bible not only answers these big questions; it offers practical advice in areas such as, How can I deal with feelings of fear or anger or guilt? How can I forgive when I cannot forget? What should I look for in a spouse? How can I have a successful marriage? How can I be a good parent? What is my spiritual gift and place in the church? What is my stewardship responsibility as a citizen? We learned the verse in Bible school, "Your word is a lamp to my feet and a light to my path" (Ps. 119:105). God's Word shows us the way forward in any area of life and on every question we face.

The Stand on the Word Bible Reading Plan takes us through the Bible chronologically. In other words, each reading takes you through the Bible as events occurred in history as far as it is possible. Here is how it works for our family. At the same time each morning, whether I am at home, in Washington, or some foreign country, I send my wife and children a morning greeting along with a reminder of the passage for the day. The text includes two questions related to the reading. The questions are designed to help in content retention, serve as an accountability tool, and provide for discussion.

The two-year plan does not have a Sunday passage. Instead, it provides an outline for a family discussion that can be done on Sunday afternoon or evening each week. The weekly discussion time begins with a spiritual leader asking each person individually for one or two insights or truths they gained from their reading during the week. After everyone else shares, you can then lead a short discussion based upon one of the passages that you read in the week just completed. It is also a time for them to ask questions.

By the way, you don't have to have all the answers. If you don't know, tell them so, then talk to your pastor or other trusted person with Bible knowledge. If your children start asking questions, that suggests they are thinking about what they are reading.

Reading God's Word will help you establish a fruitful walk with the God who made you and loves you. Whether you are single or married, this plan will enable you to lead your friends and family in daily reading God's Word. The added benefit is that you will all be reading the same text together. It will amaze you to see how God speaks sometimes in the same ways and at other times in different ways to each of you. Being on this journey together will build a spiritual synergy, a deep bond, and sense of unity and purpose like nothing else! Use it to impart the Word of life.

Appendix 2:
Prayer: Talking with God

Most Americans say they pray. But not as many pray the way Jesus did, the way He taught His disciples to pray. Fewer still really know the power in prayer God gave us to impact our families, communities, nation, and world. Prayer is our lifeline to God, our means of communicating with our heavenly Father. It develops our relationship—our friendship, fellowship, and intimacy with Him. In prayer we experience God and are "filled with the Spirit" (see Eph. 5:18–21). God uses the prayers of faithful men, women, boys, and girls to heal broken lives and strengthen families, churches, communities, and even nations. He uses our prayers to advance his Kingdom on earth (Daniel 9; Acts 4:36). He wants to use all believers!

The Essence of Prayer

Prayer is simply talking with God—about anything and everything. He is our Maker, Father, Savior, Provider, and Counselor; our Master, Healer, Guide, and Friend. Christ died for our sins and rose from the dead to sit at the right hand of God the Father, where He is praying for us right now (Heb. 10:12). His Spirit now lives within us and helps us to pray (1 John 4:16).

The Priority of Prayer

Jesus spent time alone with God regularly drawing strength from the Father and seeking His will for every decision (Luke 6:12–13; 22:39–44). His disciples asked Jesus to teach them how to pray (Luke 11:1–13). The apostles knew that prayer and obedience were the keys to Christ's life and ministry and were determined to follow His example: "[W]e will devote ourselves to prayer and to the ministry of the word" (Acts 6:4). Too few American men pray today, even pastors and leaders! Yet strong praying men are the norm in Scripture. Our families, churches, and nation need men who will make prayer a priority today! (1 Tim. 2:8).

The Practice of Prayer

Scripture teaches, "Pray continually!" (1 Thess. 5:17); "Pray always" (Eph. 6:18); "Always pray and do not give up" (Luke 18:1). Below are some helps to get you started. No one can beat the Lord's Prayer. It is an outline of key themes to guide our prayer lives: "Our Father in heaven, hallowed be your name. Your kingdom come, your will be done, on earth as it is in heaven. Give us this day our daily bread, and forgive us our debts, as we also have forgiven our debtors. And lead us not into temptation, but deliver us from evil" (Matt. 6:9–13).

In the book of Psalms and throughout Scripture, God has sprinkled prayers/patterns for us to learn from. Here is a simple, popular acronym to help jog our memories.

P-R-A-Y:

- *Praise:* Our Father which art in heaven, hallowed be thy name.
- *Repent:* And forgive us our debts, as we forgive our debtors.
- *Ask:* Give us this day our daily bread. And forgive us our debts, as we forgive our debtors. And lead us not into temptation but deliver us from evil.
- *Yield:* Thy kingdom come. Thy will be done in earth, as it is in heaven.

Praying through Scripture

God also talks to us. The Bible is His Word (2 Tim. 2:15; 3:16). Bible in hand, we should pray God's promises back to Him and claim them for our families, our work, our finances, and our nation (1 Tim. 2:1–8; 1 John 5:14–15).

Scriptures to Pray as a Man: Joshua 1:8; 1 Timothy 3:1–15; 1 Chronicles 12:32; 1 Timothy 6:1–12; 1 Corinthians 16:13; Romans 12:1–21; Micah 6:8; John 4:24; Acts 2:38: 1 Kings 2:2; Ephesians 5:25–28; Genesis 2:24; 1 Peter 3:7; Ephesians 4:26–27; Matthew 5:32; Proverbs 5:19; 1 Corinthians 6:18; Deuteronomy 4:8–10; 11:18–21; Exodus 34:5–8; Psalm 127:3–5; Matthew 7:11; Ephesians 6:4; Proverbs 22:6; Luke 11:11–12; Hebrews 12:5–7

Scriptures to Pray as a Woman: Matthew 22:36–40; Proverbs 31:30; 1 Peter 3:1–3; Ephesians 5:26; Ephesians 4:15, 29; 1 Timothy 3:11; Ephesians 5:22, 24; 1 Peter 3:1–2; Philippians 4:10–13; Philippians 2:3–4; Proverbs 31:12; 1 Corinthians 7:34; Titus 2:3–4; Titus 2:4–5; James 1:19; Ephesians 4:32; 1 Corinthians 7:1–5; Luke 2:37; Colossians 4:2; Proverbs 31:27; 1 Timothy 5:14; 1 Timothy 5:14

Scriptures to Pray for Your Children: Matthew 22:36–40; 2 Timothy 3:15; Psalm 97:10, 38:18; Proverbs 8:13; John 17:15, 10:10; Romans 12:9; Psalm 119:71; Hebrews 12:5–6; Daniel 1:17, 20; Proverbs 1:4; James 1:5; Romans 13:1; Ephesians 6:1–3; Hebrews 13:17; Proverbs 1:10–16; 13:20; 2 Corinthians 6:14–17; Deuteronomy 6; 1 Corinthians 6:18–20; Acts 24:16; 1 Timothy 1:19,4:1–2; Titus 1:15–16; Psalm 23:4; Deuteronomy 10:12; Matthew 28:18–20; Ephesians 1:3, 4:29; Ephesians 1:16–19; Philippians 1:11; Colossians 1:9; Philippians 1:9–10

Developing Personal Prayer Habits

Rise early each day to pray with opened Bible. Daniel prayed three times daily. Pray whenever you can: as you drive, with your wife, with your children at dinner and before bedtime. You cannot pray too much!

Praying Together with Others

Pray with your spouse regularly. Make time for family prayer. Be part of your church prayer meeting or group. Christ said, "My house shall be called a house of prayer" (Matt. 21:13). The apostle Paul instructed Pastor Timothy to make prayer the first order of the church, saying prayer is key to peace in the nation (1 Tim. 2:1–8). There is nothing like a Spirit-led prayer meeting with people who love the Lord! Praying women have been standing in the prayer gap for decades. Every man must set his heart to become a praying man, lead his family in prayer, and be a strong contributor to the corporate prayer life of his church. We must be leaders in praying for our morally and spiritually troubled, divided nation—and for our national leaders. American Christians simply must respond to God's promise: "If My people who are called by My name will humble themselves, and pray and seek My face, and turn from their wicked ways, then I will hear from heaven, and will forgive their sin and heal their land" (2 Chron. 7:14).

Prayer As Warfare

Jesus described the enemy, the devil, as a thief whose mission is to "steal, kill and destroy" (John 10:10). Demonic forces are at war against everything good in you, your family, your church, your community, America, and every nation (Ephesians 6:10–20).

The devil and his minions are out to thwart the kingdom of God and eliminate righteousness wherever he can. He hates God and hates people and will use spiritually ignorant and deceived men, women, boys, and girls to do his bidding. Men of God today, like the sons of Issachar in ancient Israel, need to understand the times and know what the church and our nation must do (1 Chron. 12:32). We must pull down Satan's strongholds, wrestle for our families, and use Spirit-led prayer and wisdom to help guide our churches and communities to prevail against the evil onslaught against us (2 Cor. 10:3–5). This is the war of the ages, and it is real.

Finally, Determine to Become a Person of Prayer

No matter how long you have been a Christian and may have neglected prayer up until now, you can become a person of prayer starting today. If you have missed the mark, it is not too late. Call upon the Lord, ask for His help, and proceed with His guidance. O Lord, make me a praying person; make me a prayer warrior! In Jesus's name, amen!

Book Study Discipleship Tool
To Help You Use This Book in Small Groups

Agenda

Getting Acquainted

You only get one chance to start. So having everyone there to meet one another, learn names, and connect on a "level playing field" is crucial. *Do not* be so structured in following this conversation guide you keep the Holy Spirit from moving in your group. This is intended to show you one way to navigate your time together.

Conversation Guide

The most important thing you're going to do as you start your group is *listen*! The leader who is doing all the talking is not a great small group leader!

1. What happened last week you are thankful for?
    - Everyone needs to answer briefly.
2. What challenge is happening in your life, family, or community?
    - Everyone needs to answer briefly.
3. Ask for a volunteer to pray.
    - Pray for each person by name.
    - Thank God for all the blessings on our lives.
    - Pray for the challenges we are facing.

4. Ask whether everyone was able to read the assigned chapter.
5. Ask everyone to share one main takeaway from the chapter.
6. Work through the discussion questions in the back of the chapter.
7. Once everyone has had a chance to answer the questions at the end of the chapter, complete the following:
   - Ask, "From what you have read this week and what we discussed today/tonight, what is your 'I will' statement? How are you going to apply this lesson/truth?"
   - Assign the next reading assignment/chapter for the group and confirm date and time of next meeting.
   - Ask, "Does anyone feel led to close in prayer?" If no one volunteers, the group leader will voice a short prayer and close out the group.[5]

Tips

Books

First, order the study books. Be sure to order them one month in advance from your first group meeting! It is critical that everyone leave your group on Launch Night with the book in hand.

When you realize the average American reads 2.4 books per year, you begin to grasp the potential impact reading one solid, Christian book can have on a person. And reading books in a high-accountability context is more like graduate school than reading in a recliner. Knowing you're going to be held accountable for learning the key takeaways and have a conversation with your group about the book will make the learning experience truly rich.

The best group leaders share from their own "well" of knowledge and experience, so using a book that really speaks to you is best.

Calendar

One of the most "mission critical" activities you'll do at your first session will be setting the calendar for the season. You and your group will need to decide how often you will meet as a group (weekly or biweekly) and how long you will meet. Set targets for when you will begin and end. This will prevent the meeting from taking too long (sixty to ninety minutes is ideal).

Location and Group Size

Keep the groups small. (Five is the ideal number, but four to six is okay.) Divide larger groups into subgroups and have them work through the questions simultaneously. Plan in advance the location and environment for your group. Make sure you'll have a comfortable place for everyone. Whether around a dining room table, in a den, or in another location, be sure your location is conducive to conversation and prayer. All this may help draw quiet or shy people into the discussion.

Friend and Transparency

Another important thing is friendship. You're going to need to be a *friend* to your group members. Invest in them by loving them unconditionally—this means loving them where they are, showing them you're their friend, and listening to them intently. *Transparency* is another important part of being a group leader. This book you will read together is important, and the prayer time is critical, but the real impact of a mature group leader is in sharing his life experiences, both good and bad. This is invaluable.

Pray

Praying for your group and leading your group to pray for each other are huge. Be intentional about this orienting your group to God, encouraging your group to pray for each other and for you between sessions.

Notes

1. Baba Bathra 14b–15a, Babylonian Talmud, accessed January 23, 2024, https://halakhah.com/bababathra/bababathra_14.html#PARTb and https://halakhah.com/bababathra/bababathra_15.html#15b_3.

2. This outline was adapted from a message by Adrian Rogers on this passage. Visit lwf.org.

3. Oscar C. Eliason, "Got Any Rivers," https://digitalsongsanhymns.com/songs/got-any-rivers.

4. Adrian Rogers, "The Key to Unbroken Victory," sermon, September 28, 1997, accessed January 26, 2024, https://www.lwf.org/pdfs/06_Joshua.pdf?bcs-agent-scanner=66e3d89e-a4c4-084a-a85d-b1add006dc5e, page 237.

5. These questions were chosen from Discovery Group questions that are being used globally to help catalyze Disciple-Making Movements. We acknowledge this is a different setting than the one for which they were created. Used with permission of Final Command Ministries (www.finalcommand.com).

Also available from
Fidelis Publishing and Family Research Council

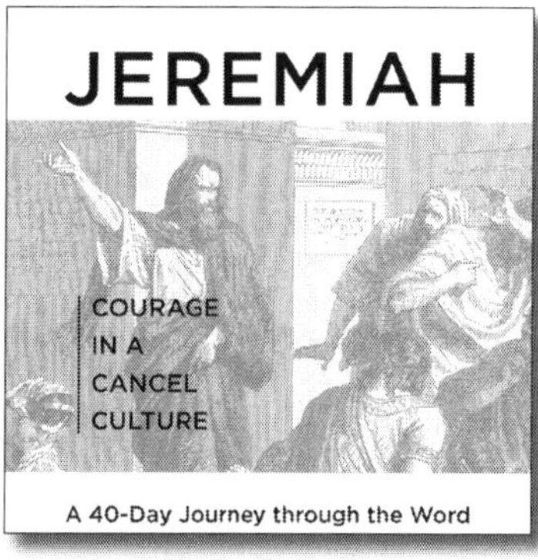

**STAND on the WORD
Study Guides and Journal**

*Jeremiah: Courage
in a Cancel Culture*
ISBN: 9781956454369

*Nehemiah:
Rebuilding a Nation*
ISBN: 9781956454468

*Ephesians:
Keep Standing!*
ISBN: 9781956454659

Stand on the Word Journal,
Volume 1
ISBN: 9781956454758